Edited by David Burton & Natasha Zdilar.

For   Helvi

National Library of Australia CiP Dewey Number
304.8940492

Almost There

Fragments of a restless Life

By Gerard Oosterman

Prologue - Those First Two Years and Own Block of Land.

So it was, after we moved from the Australian Migrant Camp of Scheyville, and in with the Van Dijks, that we discovered that their reporting about good fortunes found in Australia, were not entirely accurate. The reality of life in Australia quickly turned a sickly shade of grey. We had to put our shoulders under the tasks ahead. Mum was the chief of staff that set out on this mammoth job. Dad, was crumbling with disappointment as he was forced to accept that he would be living in the middle of a timber yard. Silently we all stood and stared at our new surrounds. Disbelief and despair settled over us as we watched huge rats getting chased by a three- legged dog, and we were further puzzled why, just like the dog, there was a 'magic' car on three wheels. Nothing made sense and it all felt quite surreal. The biggest blow however, was that the extension that was to house the eight of us had not even been built. Dad cursed the Van Dijks for their lies, and walked away from us not bothering to respond when Mum, (always the optimist) offered comfort with whatever little cheer she could muster and brightly exclaimed, 'Oh Henk, think about how lucky we are, we have the lovely cake eating after Church on Sunday.' The only thing that was true was the Van Dijks cake eating every Sunday after church. All of them hobbling downhill in the mini Renault. A coat jacket pretending to be a car.

My paternal grandparents house in Holland.

Dad just collapsed and refused to come out of bed, deeply depressed and knee-deep in gloom. Adding to his woes, the promised Government job was not available to non-British subjects. My Dad, who was totally spoon fed on life-long permanent Government security in Holland, was crushed. The temporary ideology of a culture that thrived on temporary accommodation and temporary jobs, temporary living quarters, people moving to another address at the drop of a hat, was something totally alien to us, especially Dad. He stayed in bed for six weeks.

Almost There

Fragments of a restless Life.

The beginning.

It is difficult to describe those first few years. It was difficult not to come to the conclusion that the picture of a new country as portrayed by the Australian Immigration Office in The Netherlands and the letters from the Van Dijks had not met expectations. The accommodation at the house was surrounded by a timber yard. Mud and rodents were never contemplated or talked about. The Van Dijks claim of having achieved a much better life did not really feel true. Certainly not something we would think of in terms applying to the Van Dijks. Yet, that was all we could compare with. It was odd, that our Dutch friends dating back to the war years in Rotterdam, whereby we helped each other through so many hardships, had been so deceptive in their presentation of what they had achieved in those five years in Australia. The biggest blow was not just the three-legged cars and pets, it was when we found out why the extension had not been built. They simply did not own the dilapidated house. Apart from the Sunday cake eating, there was little of substance that we, especially Dad, could find in support of the idea that Australia could make dreams come true. Perhaps the whole idea of finding a better life was based on that weekly cake eating, something that back in Holland would only occur at birthdays, at the most. Those cakes were awful though, just apple pies and mock cream. Yuk! Anyway, as stated, Mum took things in her own hand and, despite knowing hardly any English, took it upon herself to salvage our family. She dragged me and my older brother Frank around an employment agency and immediately found us work. My first wage was about 4 pounds and 5 shillings, but with overtime this could easily become 6 pounds. Frank, with his difficult behaviour and bouts of anger, would go through many jobs. It seemed as if jobs were available almost everywhere he applied. My Dad also finally got out of bed, and after a few jobs in blue overalls managed to get a technical job that he knew something about. Telephone equipment was his expertise, and he seemed happy in that it offered some security.

My introduction to work was about the time when Dad was in the middle of his six weeks bedded down with melancholy and deep depression. The pissing daughters next to the flimsy partition, the rats, the three-legged dog and the car on three wheels, took its toll. My first job was cleaning the floor of "Roger's Chains", which was a big metal-clad factory with many men working machinery making links of chains, large and small. The part that I liked most was the ordering of the factory workers lunches. Meat pies, apple pies and soft drinks. I was amazed how some of them would just eat only half and throw the rest out on the floor. I was almost tempted to eat those remnants, but did not for fear of getting infected with something horrible. The main problem was understanding the Australian accent or slang. I did notice one word that kept popping up. It seemed to get repeated almost every third or fourth word. I decided to ask the Van Dijks. What is this fukking or fucgling or fouging? You would have thought that their Dutch background would have immediately come to the rescue and explained the meaning of that word. No word in Dutch was something to be ashamed of. Sure, there are coarse words; even so, they are still just words. Instead, their five years assimilation to Australia and its culture was so successful that they immediately went into that silly Anglo world of sniggering and evasion. Was there really something so terrible going on? Was it a word so bad that one could get hung? I persisted in requesting an explanation. They finally told me that the word was bad and that it was all right for men to talk like that, but never ever in front of a woman; how curious! Not using certain words in front of a woman? What was going on here? The next bit of salient advice from the Van Dijks was to always say, beggepayrden. If you don't understand something, just say, beggepayrden. When passing someone on the bus, beggepayrden again. Well, beggepayrden, we all did. I beg your pardon!

The cleaning at Roger's Chains factory lasted just a few weeks, by which time I had earned some money which I gave to the family for saving towards accommodation and our future. I kept some which I put in a tin. My regular weekly spending was for a small packet of Craven A filter cigarettes, and the occasional orange drink called Fanta. An apple pie, just once a week, was a special treat. My next job, without even losing one day, was at another engineering factory, just a few streets behind the old job. It was run and owned by a man with just one leg. I seemed to be destined to meet creatures with missing limbs! Why was that so? Was life so fraught with accidents or danger here in Australia, that people, dogs and cars would so casually go without important parts? The owner's prosthetic leg was made of something artificial. Perhaps pine? It used to creak when he slowly walked around the factory floor. Did the leg's hinges need lubricating? His house was just in front of the factory. I sometimes used to see the wife. She was very prim and proper and polite; content to mind the petunias in the front garden. She kept well away from the factory. If only she knew? The factory shenanigans and 'dating' she would not have liked! The owner always had a cigarette hanging from his mouth which made the (bad) word 'fucking' even more sinister sounding. The F seemed to go on forever. Hissing with spittle as a lubricant. He did obey the rule, though, of never saying that in front of his wife.

L-R: Mum, Mr. van Dijk, Dad, John, Dijk's daughter Lisbeth, Mrs.van Dijk, Adrian

The job of cleaning the factory floor was sometimes relieved by learning to work on machinery, a capstan lathe and milling machines, making nuts or bolts, putting threads on them. In fact, a bit of skill was creeping into my daily routine. In the meantime, I had saved for an old bicycle and this enabled me to save bus money by travelling to and from work by bike.

The job was not what I had intended to do when still back in Holland. I had some vague idea of studying to become an aircraft engineer. Sweeping a factory floor and buying lunches for factory workers was not all that inspiring. Nor was the blatant homosexual capers that used to be played out very edifying. The non-stop pretend buggering was endemic, and the tolerance towards it staggering. Here was a really curious bit of factory culture. Most of the adult workers were married, had families, or if not married, spoke about their girlfriends. Yet, it was almost as if all that homosexual pretend buggering was proof of being heterosexual. To not partake in it, as I refused to do, was considered to be sissy. The social gatherings at that time showed similar traits. To be with women at a party was seen as having 'poofter' inclinations. You would not want to be seen with the opposite sex as this was being 'soft' and not masculine. Perhaps it again had something to do with the acute shortage of women during those penal times some decades before. Many just had to do with what was available, and that was each other, and of the same sex. Old habits die hard. Another habit was to stick fingers up an unexpected worker's bum through overalls or apron. It was called 'dating'. The owner of the second factory and wooden leg had a curious way of dealing with others. His mouth did not just contain a fag with brown spittle leaking, but his mouth was also set permanently at twenty past eight o'clock. He would spend the day creaking around the factory floor with his gammy leg, sneering and leering at the cavorting going on. At times he would get into his strides and gun for me. He would grab my hair and pull my head towards the floor. 'You forgot this bit here,' he would say, 'look at it, you bastard, here,' and he would spit a lifetime of smoking induced phlegm onto the floor. Those unfortunate experiences were tolerated when considering that the payoff was not having to join in any buggering in front of the Capstan lathe machine.

My Dad's parents wedding photo at the Krasnapolski Hotel in Amsterdam

Again, at some time later and another job, I was an apprentice spectacle maker in Clarence Street, Sydney. The initiation for the young and upcoming workforce was for the adults to get ultra-marine blue or cobalt blue dye in powder form. After taking down the pants of the uninitiated, they would rub this powdered dye around the genitals of the hapless victim. This dye was so strong it would stain legs, genitals and clothes for weeks. Later on, when I found out that this was widespread and tolerated as an almost essential part of 'growing up', I knew that there was a serious and serial kind of bullying going on. Of course, at that time I was also astonished to observe young kids going to schools in quasi-army uniforms and with mock rifles slung over their tiny shoulders. They were cadets. Was there a war still? Girls, in the middle of hot summers with black skirts, black tops, black hats, black stockings and even black gloves. Was there some connection between all that and bullying? My younger brothers and single sister were enrolled at different schools. Some at the primary school locally, and two brothers at a catholic high school, called 'De La Salle' College. It was not long before our parents found out that the punishment of whacking her children with a ruler or cane was not all that rare. So, off the 'chief of staff' (Mum) went to confront the Head Brother of this 'benevolent' College, wanting to stop the bullying by physical violence of her children. The practice that was commonly used would be the voluntary holding up of the palm of hands, whereby the kindly 'Un-Christian Brother' would sweep down at full throttle and hit the upturned palm with the ruler. Another much liked version was the hitting of hands with the knuckles up. This was popular because it inflicted so much more pain, and was even more effective in installing subservience and non-questioning education in pupils.

Another perplexing insight in this new country was given that for children to move up to the next level of education, it did not actually depend on having passed examinations on subjects, but rather on how much someone had grown taller. The younger ones did not have the advantage that Frank and I had of having had a few years of English back in Holland, so it was perhaps much harder during those first couple of years for the younger brothers and sister to stay in front. When it was suggested that John should perhaps spend another year at the same level, the answer was that John was so tall he could not possibly spend another year in the same class. So, there you have it. The assimilation took some time, getting used to all those differences, but we were doing not too bad. The young ones soon started coming home with English phrases, which in turn gave my Mum the opportunity to pick up the lingo. Amazingly, Mum, who had barely gone through high school back in Holland, was without fear when it came to practicing her new language. She did better than Dad, who was more circumspect and less accepting of all that Aussie slang and strangeness. He was amazed seeing elderly ladies who had 'blue hair'. Once he came home and, I will never forget it, he said, 'I saw a woman with pink hair today'. Oh, those differences! After perhaps a year or so with the Van Dijks, the three-legged-rat-chasing dog and Chevy-pickup patiently waiting on bricks for its relief in rubber, it was time to move on.

Enough money had been saved, and many weekends were spent looking for our own block of land. We had, by now, met several other Dutch couples with children and their own block of land. Some blocks even had a temporary dwelling on it. This was very much the talk at social gatherings. Indeed, some of those had already found the block and had moved from Migrant Camp or rented accommodation into their own temporary dwelling. Let me explain that "own block" is a block of sub-divided land with its own title that could be bought. In Australia, then as now, the dream of owning a block of land had reached an almost religious fervour amongst the just arrived migrant. The talk was contagious, and after coming home from an afternoon of talk with others about this possibility of having our own block, we were beside ourselves with the prospect of having a large garden where we could play or perhaps keep a dog with four legs and have leghorn chickens. After having looked for a few weeks, the block with 'temporary dwelling' was found. Hoorah. It was near a railway, had a small shopping Centre, and was also in the process of building a pub with a modern circular roof line. It was the buzz of Sydney, a pub with a domelike structure. We really had landed with our nose in the butter. This suburb was Revesby. The most important aspect of this search for our own block of land was that requirement to be near a railway station. Sydney already then had expanded over a very large area with a centre around the Harbour Bridge and Town Hall. A cobweb of rail lines was going in all directions and to many dozens of suburbs. They were spread out to perhaps fifteen kilometres or more from the centre. The further one went, the cheaper the land. However, if the land was near a rail station that would be regarded as a significant advantage. A premium would be paid for the convenience. So, the choice was, either close to the city but pay more, or further out but near a rail line and pay less or the same. The land near the city was often hard to find, but also much smaller in area and far more congested with people and cars, noise and smoke.

Our move from the Van Dijks to our Revesby block was by a truck that moved the gleaming chrome plated bunk beds and all the bits and pieces that had been sent over from Holland. A dressoir or dresser with a mirror, also some chairs and a coffee table was about the bulk of it. It also included the 'lazy chair' which had an adjustable back that could be slotted to a more horizontal level for comfort, with arm rests which were wide enough to support an ashtray. This is where Dad used to sit and ponder, and smoke his ciggies. The laden truck left in the afternoon. I remember Dad helping to prevent the scattering of household items along Woodville Road by spreading himself eagle-like on top of sloping boxes of pots and pans at the back. The arrival at our own block and temporary dwelling went smoothly, and things were put inside our fibro-asbestos dwelling.

Life on the merry go round in Australia's suburb, with my sister and two brothers.

The sleeping of the eight of us needed the ingenuity of creators of puzzles. How to fit all of us in an area of 8 by 4 meters? Simple, piece of cake! Stack all mattresses during the day and put them all down during the evening and night. The turning around at night during sleep had to be carefully stage managed, and restless sleep was not allowed. This went on for a few weeks when, after saving up for bags of cement, sand and blue metal, a concrete base was poured for an extension to the fibro garage. The cement, sand and blue metal was hand mixed and a floor of 8 by 3 meters was poured. The week after, Mr. V.Dijk, who, as previously mentioned, had building experience, knocked together the extension with a timber frame and clad it with the asbestos cement sheeting externally and corrugated asbestos roof sheets. The living space had now increased a massive 50% and all boys slept in the extension, with our sister, Dora, and parents in the original dwelling. Dad knocked a hole in the wall to gain excess to the 'bedroom'. As it turned out, the roof sheeting had not been long enough and the extension leaked whenever it rained, which made sleeping on the top bunks a wet experience. Not to worry, a plastic sheet was fastened above the top bunks and to the roof timbers so the water would run on top of the sheet and then down the inside of the wall and seep out into the soil. The earth was outside, but only just!

The sleeping arrangement. Brother John at the front. My Parents in a single bed. My sister Dora on the floor. Herman and Adrian above and below my parents on both sides, and Frank who is smiling on the top bunk. The empty matrass is mine taking the photo.

The First Two Years.

We lived in that dwelling for over two years. Frank had managed to go through so many jobs it was getting more obvious as time went by, that there was a problem that could no longer be ignored. Our dwelling was not lined inside. This meant that we were separated from the outside by just 5 millimetres of the asbestos cement sheeting. The heat in summer and the frost in winter were never far away, particularly the winters were somewhat worse than we had imagined. At no stage did we ever contemplate that Australia could be cold, let alone have frost. All we ever saw were tropical gardens and waving palm trees. A peculiar incident that we experienced of Australian easy going culture, occurred when Mum had to be hospitalized for a couple of weeks. She had those mysterious stays in hospitals occasionally. Perhaps it was woman trouble or varicose vein disturbances. I never really found out, but considering she only died a few years ago at the sound age of 96, I feel that her health overall was well taken care of. During the first few months on our own block with dwelling, we had knocked up some kind of chicken pen. John had gone to the city markets, called Paddy Markets, and came home with six leghorns travelling by train. The chooks were carried in a hessian bag with their heads sticking out of holes specifically made for breathing purposes. The train was crowded and had standing place only. John had no option but to stand in the area between carriages and hold onto a post with one hand and the bag of chooks above his head with the other. Fellow travellers were being entertained by being stared upon by the beady eyes of the somewhat nervous leghorns above.

So, back to the peculiar incident. During the hospital period we were given a domestic help from the government, or perhaps the local church. She was in her late fifties, and one of those old girls that looked as if she would play bingo and frequent the ladies lounge at the local pub. She was bone idle but as kind as a raffle ticket. Her main job was to cook and prepare an evening meal when all kids and Dad would be home. The routine was simple; lamb-chops, spuds and boiled vegetables. Later on, we were told by neighbours, during the day she would saunter up to the Revesby pub (with the round dome) and have 'a couple' before coming back and preparing the meal... Her specialty, however, was the dessert. This dessert was a very sweet fruit mince type of cake, a bit like a Christmas type pudding, but, and this is amazing, she had taken the rounded domed water dish from the chook pen to make the cake in. It must have had the perfect shape for the cake! Now we knew what happened to the water dish. Each time the dish was returned to the chooks she would, without as much as batting her eyelids, take the dish back to make yet another cake. To make sure the chickens were not without water, she would put a normal saucepan in the pen. As it turned out, most of the young leghorns turned out to be roosters. No eggs. Was this another variant on the three-legged creatures? Many times, when the kids came home from school, she would be found snoring away enjoying an alcohol induced nap.

At the time of the leghorns, John also bought a sweet little Labrador puppy from the same city markets at the back of Central Station towards Ultimo. This was quite a busy place on a Saturday. All the rural producers and markets gardeners would get to the city markets and sell their wares. Most of those behind the stalls were Italian, Greek and different Russian Federation vendors, also some Baltic or 'Balts,' as they were called. The best, freshest and cheapest vegetables could be bought there. Many of the customers were also Europeans, not just buying the vegetables or livestock, but also for the 'life' itself. At the time of our arrival in 1956, the only place to get coffee, as opposed to that dreadful invention Nescafe with the 43 beans, was to go to either David Jones or Paddy's markets. Worse, once in a cafe we asked if the coffee served was real, and the answer was to point to the large powdered instant coffee tin. The waitress at that time did not know that coffee came from beans.

Soon after John came home with the previously mentioned Labrador puppy, tragedy struck him. How tragedy can strike at a young age is what we are supposed to accept as part of growing up. It is how we 'deal with it,' we are told much later on. At some stage, with disappointments and the mystery of everlasting magic waning, we grow up a little wiser, but also a little less feeling young and protected from life's misery. The puppy, after John built a nice dog house and spent his pocket money on leads and special puppy food, became ill with fatal distemper. It lasted a number of weeks. John held out hope till the very end and would sit up all day and night in the garden with his beloved but very sick puppy. It finally died. John was heaving with grief; he loved the chickens, but much more his puppy. He was inconsolable. After a suitable period of grieving and getting over this blow, he came up with his next animal project, homing pigeons. We had some experience with homing pigeons at our top floor place at The Hague. During the last year or so of our stay in Holland, both John and I built a pigeon loft on the large balcony outside. The pigeons were those lovely racing pigeons that serious breeders would take to other countries and release. The pigeon that came home first would win a prize. This is how I understood it at the time. We had bought our first pigeons from a school friend not far from our street. We generally liked the flying of pigeons coming back to their loft for feed and were fascinated by their homing instincts. From those early pigeon memories that are still with me, most of the pigeons we had bought, when released, would immediately return to their previous owner. The owner, for a small cost, would give them back. He was running a lucrative business in selling pigeons that were old and probably trained to always come back to their owners, and then sell over and over the same homing pigeons.

Own House on Our Own Block.

The building of our own house started after about two years of living in the asbestos sheeted garage, euphemistically named by Shire Councillors a, 'temporary dwelling'. You were not allowed to live in a garage, but if the garage was named 'temporary dwelling' all was fine, and hundreds of thousands of migrants would start their life in Australia living inside those small dwellings. It was the leg-up to something grander in the future, namely 'own home on our own block'. After months of handwringing, worrying about paying interest and taking a loan, and endless negotiations with several lenders, it was decided to accept a loan from The Dutch Building Society. The rate of interest, a ridiculous 2 or 3 percent for the building of a home. Many home-plans were looked at and a final three bedroom plan was chosen. The bricks for the foundation footings were laid. I jumped from footing to footing and remember thinking that the house appeared rather small. Soon after, the rest of the material arrived, including a large pile of red cement roof tiles. A few broke unloading from the truck. Dad thought it an immediate disaster.

Within a couple of months the house was built, painted and handed over. We moved from our cramped temporary dwelling to a more generous sized house. The house was small but had three bedrooms and a bathroom with shiny Masonite based wall panelling that had some kind of tile effect embossed on it. The floor had real mosaic type tiles, quite pretty and practical. There was a hand-basin and a hot and cold shower and bath, but no toilet because at that time there still was no sewerage connected in most of the outer suburbs of Sydney. Mum was pleased with the house, and her dream of having a bathroom had finally been fulfilled. Not having sewerage connected was normal in Australia during the time of European immigration from early days till the early 1960's. The enormous distances between houses and suburbs, and the sheer spread of just a few hundred people over many kilometres of land, made the provision of infrastructure such as sewerage systems too expensive for the time. The way out was for the local Council to provide a 'dunnee-pan'. This pan was a heavy metal container coated with pitch or bitumen. It had a fresh smell. A bit like an industrial harbour foreshore. Moorings and thick ropes, tarred anchors and pylons! The fresh smell was always of short duration. This pan would be used in a small outside room of about two square meters and called the 'dunnee'. Sometimes politely called by the rich of the upper north shore, 'the out-house'… The dunnee pan would be covered by another outer metal shell with a hinged wooden lid. With some imagination, this could then be seen as a toilet. However, when lifting the lid, no matter what it looked like from the outside, the smell and darkness inside was brutally brooding and very sienna-brown. It left nothing at all to the imagination. Not too many would linger or write poetry or read 'The Catholic Weekly.' The pan would be collected once a week by burley blokes in blue singlets and verdant armpits, who would come before dawn and summer-heat, to heave the full sloshing pan on shoulders and put it on a truck. Coarse oaths would be renting the still morning air and heavily shod feet would crunch the concrete path along the side of the veranda. This dunnee pan would be capped by a lid secured on top with some sort of metal band that would lever the lid tightly around the container, not unlike some preservatives, such as sauerkraut or apple sauce, of the present day. This was a job purely reserved for dinky-di Australians and much coveted. It was well-paid and had all sorts of lurks, including dalliances with lonely women and early knock off times when finished. I am not sure if the smell added to their appeal, but rumours had it that many a woman, widowed, single or even married, were left happy after an early visit from the 'dunnee man'. Large families were given a 'special two pan treat'. This usually meant giving very generously to the dunnee man at Christmas time (a couple of crates of beer would suffice). Any large family that were too stingy at Christmas would soon find a lonely single pan again. Those dunnee men were often kind rogues but a law onto their own. They were revered by many and feared by some. The 'dunnee man' is now part of folklore and long gone since.

Our family was more than just large, and Dad had to make some adjustment to a down gutter pipe outside the dunnee. It would carry rain water from the roof to the open storm water drain at the front of the street. Despite our generosity towards the Shire's dunnee men at Christmas time, we never had more than two pans a week. For our family this was not enough. I never did find out how our neighbours coped, they had six children as well. We were on friendly terms, but not that friendly that you could ask, what do you do with your shit? In any case, their concern was more focused on the fan tail pigeons' shit on their shiny roof tiles all caused by my brother John's flock of sixty pigeons... It would have been unwise to mention anything to do with poo. It was not as if our family produced too much solid stuff. No, it was the sloshing around of the liquid waste that was the problem. Of course, being right next to neighbours it wasn't as if one could go outside at any time and urinate in the garden. This is what happened though. When the height in the pan became critical, and the dunnee man still a day or so away from collecting, Mum told us to do as much urinating as possible at school or wait till late at night and then in the garden in the dark. In the summer, this caused some olfactory concerns, and when this ammonia-like stench could no longer be hidden or blamed on Dad's fertilizer for the veggie patch, Dad did a piece of engineering that is still admired to this day. As I already said, there was a metal downpipe running on the outside of the toilet that carried rainwater from the roof to the trench at the front of the house. Dad simply cut a small hole in the fibro on the inside of the toilet directly abutting the down pipe and conveniently next to the pan. This hole was also made on the inside of the downpipe. Both holes synchronized brilliantly. This square hole was then used for all the males (six in total) as a urinal. The piss went straight down the downpipe and to the front of the house in the open storm water trench. This trench was usually overgrown with weeds. Generous rains would wash it downhill and finally into concrete storm-water and into the Georges River. The Council used to come along three times a year to get rid of the weeds and mow the grass around it. Well, our trench was the most luxuriously green and lush looking of the whole street. It would have won a blue ribbon for excellence if that nature strip could have been entered into the Sydney Agricultural Easter Show. It wasn't till many years later that sewerage was connected and my Mum's dream of her 'own bathroom' with inside flushing toilet was truly fulfilled. My Dad was a genius.

Those First Years.

In Revesby, I had developed different interests, was working, and had bought a Lambretta Scooter with money saved up. John, who was still at school and sad with the loss of his beloved puppy, thought he would at least have some involvement with animals. The roosters were useless and fought tooth and nail when they grew up. John, the eternal optimist, would not believe that all were roosters, and waited until the crowing started. They were subsequently given a shovel and buried. The chicken coup was transformed into a pigeon house. After yet another trip to Paddy's market, and another hessian bag on the train, John came home with some pigeons. The racing pigeons were in the sack together with some really lovely 'fan-tails'. They were white and used to fan their tail feathers out when in an amorous mood. Pigeons are often amorous, and as a result John soon had a couple of dozen pigeons. The inbreeding or line breeding of the birds was no hindrance, and the resulting progeny certainly did not suffer from any genetic malfunctions. They continued unabated with the same amorous behaviour and vigour. Soon John had sixty or more. Their homing instincts were superb, and eating them would have been considered pet murder. The sky for the birds was their limit. The chicken coup was the home for the night, but during the day, they would happily do the rounds between the shiny suburban neighbours' rooftops. They enjoyed sitting on top, and when bored did some more couplings. They took turns sitting on eggs.

The pride and joy of our neighbours were their gleaming houses. Many a Saturday would be spent sprucing and brushing the exterior of their homes. The gardens also were meticulously kept. Not a leaf would be allowed to rest on roof or lawn. The neighbour right next to us, Bill, with a lovely wife and six children, would spend entire weekends on knees, tending his lawn. At first, I thought he was praying or perhaps meditating, even though at that time the art of meditation was decades away. Later on, I discovered, while carefully and discretely looking at his kneeling down, he was having a small fork-like tool whereby he would crawl around the lawn and dig out bits of undesired grass. I have never ever discovered what the aim was. I can only surmise that he wanted a uniform lawn without the intrusion of different green blades of grass that did not belong to the specie that he so badly desired in his lawn. He would sometimes stand up, straighten himself, and roll a cigarette. He was then a picture of contentment, only to cloud over when looking at John's pigeons on his roof. His work to make the perfect lawn was interrupted by John's pigeons. The pigeons were hell-bent on roosting on his shiny red terra cotta tiled roof. The house was new and pigeons did not respect this, or were totally unaware of the owner's pride in trying to preserve the house, almost as if still in wrapping or gift paper. They, the pigeons, especially the fan-tails, shat unrelentingly and in total irreverence to Bill, the neighbour. The cooing by the many pigeons, which was music to John's ears, sounded to Bill like a war cry, a kind of bugle heralding an army of defecators ready to defile his pride and joy, his terra-cotta roof. For years, the good humoured Bill would climb on the roof, and with a stiff broom sweep off the white pigeon shit. Of course, it would all roll into his gutter, which meant he also had to clean them out. He was as particular with his roof as he was with his lawn. To his credit, he would sometimes allude to the pigeon problem but was too good natured to make a fuss. It was only after we built our own house that our Dad thought the pigeons should go. They had now taken a fancy to our new roof and the numbers were becoming unmanageable.

Earlier Times.

The photo above was taken on Meindert Muller's parents' property that had fruit trees. I don't know much more than the fruit trees, but it must have taken hold because apart from that, I can't remember anything else. I was just two years old. Holland had capitulated two years before and Germany was now running Holland. The worst was yet to come. When I told my Mum many years later how I remembered her cooking something on one of those pump primus little heater/stoves one very early and frosty morning, she was amazed because I was just two years old. She was cooking some porridge before taking me somewhere to a distant relative who still had more food than us. He was a tailor, married but no children. On the way there, my Mum pulled me along on a snow sledge. The uncle lived some kilometres away. While she pulled me along, she spotted some German soldiers coming our way. She quickly pulled sledge and me into a ditch hoping they hadn't noticed us. We kept hidden till they walked past. They had either not noticed us or were just not bothered. The primus was a solid baked enamelled green cooking device. As was our green bucket that we kept the milk in. Saucepans, too, were enamelled and lasted for years, lifetimes even. When they developed a hole, a special man used to go around and patch them up. Everything was patched up, restored and fixed. Now we chuck it out and rivers are full of debris choking up reeds, dams and trees during flooding rain. I spotted a perfectly good travel case stuck high up a tree during last week's rain. I assumed it was in good order because that's how it is. We buy new not because the old has worn or broken, but because that's how consumerism works. It has got us in its magic spell.

The peak of my early teen years was having discovered the roseate softness of budding breasts and smouldering hot eyes in a lovely and eager girl. I was full of wonder. What else there was still to discover. Her name was Margo. All this rudely interrupted with my parents' decision to go so insanely far away. I had to live off those fleeting memories with Margo for a very long time after! The Australian suburban dullness never quite managed to wipe the good memories away. Of course, 'the best times of my life' should not be taken too literally. Times of unlimited possibilities and boundless optimism and belief in everything and nothing is experienced by most, but perhaps all too briefly during those teenage years. Later on it changes and seriousness so easily takes over for many. A routine becomes the enemy but I can say that I have been somewhat successful in fighting this routine and dulling repeats. I never did become an insurance actuary or dedicated estate agent. Lacking a burning ambition in following a single profession was my forte. But how is one to know what profession to follow? I did have a period whereby I suffered from not going to work wearing a suit. I seemed to do jobs always wearing overalls or just work-wear with steel- capped boots. I had fantasies of gaining some importance and recognition or worth by going to work in a proper suit. If possible, I would carry an attaché case with important papers. I returned to Holland and achieved this by working for a bank. I wore a suit for a few months. It wasn't at all what I thought it would be. In the tram (line 22 to East Amsterdam) no one took notice and it was a lonely time in the office. No recognition or any importance at all. I did learn some book-keeping and typing.

After a few trips backwards and forwards, an escape from Dutch National Service and the bank job with suit, I ended up coming good after all. I married Helvi in Finland, who I had met a year or more before while skiing in Austria. She was still studying and I was painting pictures. It was a long time ago.

This photo of me in Holland (middle) pondering, during one of the best times of my life.

All Aboard To Australia.

Let's now move forward, or back to, (depending on what you might have read so far), to my parents' decision to migrate. The first murmurs I heard involved Argentina followed by South Africa. Australia came about because some war-time friends (the Van Dijks) had already taken the step in the very early fifties. It took nine days to fly to Australia. Their choice had been Australia. Many letters were exchanged and they were of the most euphoric kind. The streets of Australia were paved in gold and all was possible, own cars, own homes, cake eating on Sunday with mountains of cream, you name it, Australia had it all. My Mum was really taken in by it with prospects of our own home more than anything, and especially with a bathroom.

The planning stage evolved rapidly with a visit to the Australian embassy and inspection by an Australian Doctor. X- Rays were taken and the basics of our health determined by standing around in underpants while chests were listened to by the doctor. We were asked to turn this way and that way. We had to touch toes and stick our tongues out to the Doctor. All our vaccinations were always strictly adhered to. Soon we all were deemed to be fit for Australia. We were the perfect white family for migrating, and as there were six of us, Australia must have been drooling.

Here a quick look again at those earlier war time periods. I seem to be joking or having fun still... Thirteen years later and I would find myself in Australia. It took a while for 'fun' to surface again.

The Author in wooden clogs

We finally walked through the canvas hooded walkway to our ship. The gateway to five weeks on-board, a luxury boat full of Dutch migrants. Bye, bye Holland. There was a little band on board that would play over and over, 'it was on the isle of Capri that I found her, with 'O' Sole Mio' after we left Genoa. All hell broke loose when the boat pulled away from Sicily's Messina. Many of those sons of Italian families would never be seen back again in those ancient villages. The Mums left behind would be milling together, shedding tears around the water-wells for many years yet. The journey away from shores and love, so sadly final and permanent. A return impossibly expensive, and at the time would not have been contemplated. Luigi, the best cobbler in Palermo now gone. So was Antonio the dressmaker's son. When the boat pulled away from Amsterdam and harbour, my Mum and Dad must have felt that too, but with six of us needing to find our allocated cabins, they soon kept busy.

Bye-bye, Holland, forever.

Frank (tall) with Herman on his left, Dora on right with Adrian just before leaving Dutch Port.

I took the next photo with my newly bought camera earned from delivering fruit and vegetables to Embassies at The Hague in the many weeks before migration (mainly from American Embassy tips, which were extraordinarily generous, and with hot soup as well).

The time on board was amazing, a holiday as never before. Can you imagine getting a new menu to choose from each time? The decisions to make; pork or beef, chicken, and in morning, eggs boiled or fried? There was table tennis, a sweep stake which we always won some money with. And that little orchestra; 'It was on the Isle of Capri that I found you.' The Italians were still doe-eyed and so sad!

Freemantle in 1956 on Sunday.

The two weeks travelling from Aden to Freemantle was mainly spent watching my parents getting their luggage trunks from down in the bowels of the ship up deck to make an inventory and ensure we would all be ready for Sydney. My parents wanted us to make a good impression in Australia and only Sunday best would do. The arrival in Freemantle was on a Sunday. I have to go back a few months now. A good friend told me; tell your parents to think twice before going to Australia. It is a very boring country and on Sunday everything is closed. The arrival in Freemantle on a Sunday proved his warning to be correct. The only people walking around were the passengers from the boat. It was something like out of the Neville Shute book and film, 'On the Beach,' that was yet to be made. All of us looking at each other, all of us dressed in our Sunday-best with proper coats and ties, cleanly scrubbed necks and underpants. But, what for? Freemantle was empty, or at least it looked empty. I did hear a cricket score filtering through the blinds, not that I knew what a cricket score was then.

The Arrival in Sydney; Dreams, Chevy Pick-up and Nightmares

After the ship's berth in Sydney we were greeted by our Dutch friends. They had already gone through all those emotions and experiences that we were now bravely facing head-on. My Dad looked tense while greeting our friends. Our war-time friends and previous neighbours from Rotterdam were seasoned and well-adjusted migrants, who, according to the letters they sent us, were totally happy and content with having made that choice so many years earlier. There were also many others greeting the new arrivals, holding up signs with 'carpenters, painters, bricklayers wanted.' It was as if one could already start earning money within minutes of landing. Was this a sign of, 'In Australia, streets are paved with gold?'

Dad must have arranged for our trunks of belongings to be forwarded to Scheyville migrant camp that we were supposed to travel to. The original plan to stay and live with our friends were put on hold. The reason I heard was, if we could first knuckle down to camp life, we would be better equipped and appreciate living with our Dutch friends afterwards. I think that might have well been the reason for my Dad's previously mentioned furrowed tense look. Did he smell a rat?

The photo below might be one of the first taken after arrival in Sydney. We are still on board. Dad and Mum must have been frantically packing the cases and organizing all the luggage. What a job and with six children. Notice our Sunday best attire including ties and coats! It would have been hot in February, even so, a good impression on arrival was to be persevered with. Mum told us to wet our hair and run a comb through it. I always did try to get a slight wave at the front of my too straight hair with the help of a generous blob of brilliantine. I had my own jar. The onshore stevedoring workers were dressed in blue singlets and shorts. They could well have thought, while looking up and rolling their ready-rub ciggie; 'Here comes another bloody boatload of bloody reffos.' Definition of 'reffo' was 'a refugee.' Strictly speaking, we were not refugees, but we were all painted with the same brush. European history was complicated, and Australians at that time kept things fairly simple. At least we were white.

Me, Adrian and John after landing in Sydney 1956

I remember taking the next photo (and developing it). It would have been after our stay at the migrant camp. The woman with the perm was called aunty but wasn't a real aunt at all, more like a fierce dragon. She used to lock Frank and John up in the coal shed when they had done a number two in their pants during the war and at their Montessori kindergarten. I had to walk both my brothers home to this so called aunty. Mum was in hospital giving birth or something. Doing number two's during war time wasn't unusual. In fact, it was one of those things that at least gave some relief during times of extreme trauma and bombs.

L-R: Mum, Dutch friend's daughter, brothers Frank, Adrian and Herman. Then Mrs van Dijk, (Late) brother John with daughter of friend.

Our friends came to greet us at Sydney's port not in their much talked about American car, but instead they travelled by train. A bit of a blow, considering how much they boasted about it, but it was just the first day. We walked around Sydney with them and that's when I enjoyed my first milkshake. In Holland, I drank milk and had never imagined one could better the taste of cow's milk by shaking it and mixing it with an unguent such as strawberry or vanilla. But, there you have it. A country of milk and honey, the milkshake was just the beginning. The milk-bar had a strange name, probably 'Stavros' or even 'Mavros Milk bar.' It was in George Street but not anymore.

At midday we had to say goodbye to our friends as the buses were now ready to take us well outside Sydney to our Migrant Camp, Scheyville.

Scheyville Camp.

Soon we were all packed in a convoy of buses and heading towards our migrant camp, Scheyville. My milkshake and sandwiches bedded down, the adventure and first glimpses of Australia would now roll past. Those first images were vital, and I hope the remembering is as truthful as possible. Did those fleeting images already set in motion future opinions and possible prejudices of Australia? Was I seeing my first glimpses of future resentments? I really can't answer that. As a fifteen year old, I would have been bursting with excitement in seeing a foreign country. There can't be any doubt about that!

We had already seen Fremantle and Melbourne. Fremantle was on a Sunday. Sundays in Australia during the fifties were expected to be spent on reflections of Mum England and caring for lawns. Melbourne did have people about and we took a train trip to the inner city. The train carriages were made of wood, and so were many of the cars. I could not believe the age of the cars, they seemed out of a world of my meccano set, given by my Parents a couple of years before migration.

My parents before any children in Holland. A great picture of happy life, contentment. (Why did they go to Australia?) I don't know what that board was in her lap. It could have been a crocheting work in progress. My Mum was always doing something. Idleness was not in her. Glad to see the grass was unkempt. Dad seems dreamily serious.

As our bus took off, it soon found its way on a very busy road. I noticed large signs and many car sales yards with car bonnets open, as if yawning or waiting to be fed. Later on, I found out the road was called Parramatta Road. About an hour along the journey, the bus stopped and the driver walked across the road and disappeared into a pub. He left us baking inside the bus. So what? It just allowed the passengers to see more carefully of much that was new and different while the driver downed a couple of beers. Within a few months I noticed that beer drinking was very popular, as long as it was done before six PM. Pubs closed at six, allowing husbands to get home, and if possible hand over the pay-packet before it all got pissed up against the porcelain. It is a hot and harsh country and beer does alleviate it.

When we arrived at Scheyville we were more or less abandoned. There was someone who gave us a number for our accommodation. We had no clue as to what to expect. No film footage at The Hague Embassy ever showed us converted metal corrugated Nissan Huts to be for many migrants and refugees the first form of accommodation. We just saw coloured films of postmen jumping fences giving glad tidings to very happy home owners standing tall on the well-manicured lawns. Everyone beaming with happiness. All wearing gleaming white teeth in total sympathy with white picket fences. The same with newspapers being chucked onto the same front lawns. It all seemed so very unregimented and free, so jolly and sunny.

As we found our accommodation corresponding with our given number, it was a surprise to be shown ex-army huts. Nissan huts, to be precise. This looked much regimented and was totally without smiles. Mum said, "Oh, this must be for our bikes," grabbing her first impression, hoping against all odds this wasn't for sleeping in, surely not! Her Dutch-ness escaped momentarily into a second of desperation. In Holland, of course, a bicycle is part of all life. Why not here as well? But why would bicycles have mattresses and chairs?

Within a few minutes reality set in, but my Mum immediately accepted and got busy settling in. She was the hero of all migration, and should have been given a Dame-hood, surely? We had suitcases with the basics and soon had our bedding arrangement sorted out. The bedside drawers had some crusts of bread in them. Later on, we met a Dutch couple who had been in exactly the same hut just before us and had abandoned the bread in the drawers. We laughed heartily about that for many years to come. (It wasn't all sad.)

The above photo of my parents standing on one the quays of Sydney harbour. I have some doubt of when this photo was taken. Was it on the day of arrival? Why is that man at the front clapping his hands? Is he applauding Australia? My Dad (bald head) seems to be a bit bewildered. The lady with the handbag is my Mum. In any case, all seem happy!

Europe on Mutton Chops at Scheyville Camp.

The first night in the Nissan hut would have been spent in a deep slumber. It was all so much to take in. We must have been exhausted. The long hot bus drive along miles of car yards, huge hoardings of Vincent's APC's headache powders, the beer stop-over, the unloading and dispersion of all into the low-slung huts of Scheyville Camp, had all been bravely taken in our stride. An overload of emotions. My parents would perhaps have had some thoughts of Holland. Life back then was so orderly. Life on-board a Dutch passenger liner was still a bit like being in Holland, but

Scheyville was not. Today we might well have said, 'far out.' The following weeks I did not take any photos. Perhaps feelings of ambiguity about Australia were rising already, or was I merely reflecting or responding to my Dad's visible distress? I am not sure. It was so long ago. I know that no photos were taken till we went to live with our Dutch war-time friends. Frank, John and I were too busy scanning the grounds and immediate surroundings. It was hot and very humid with regular torrential downpours on most afternoons. The countryside was rain flooded with hills sticking up like islands, bleating cattle atop, looking around for help. We also noticed in the distance, trees with oranges suspended from their branches. They looked inviting. Can one imagine oranges hanging there just like in the Garden of Eden? With the camp isolated and marooned we were somewhat stuck, and mud was everywhere, including on our shoes. Poor

Dad could not cope with this new experience of mud on shoes and flew into a fit of anger. Even though Holland was the country that had invented rain, mud on shoes was unheard of. We were city kids. There was simply no mud in The Hague (only embassies giving generous tips). Dad was coping the best he could, but mud on his shoes was one step too far, especially then!

An unforgettable memory etched in my mind was the generosity of the Australian government run camp with the availability of unlimited supplies of food. It was all free and copious in quantity. The first few days we ate in the very large food hall. You picked up the food by queuing at the kitchen counter with a large plate. You ate what was ladled out. It was mainly enormous mutton chops, still glistening in fat with peas and a mountain of mashed potatoes. Sometimes it was sausages and pumpkin. You then carried the full plate back to large tables that had knives and forks already spread out. You sat on benches. We would all tuck in with a vengeance.

You can imagine, most migrants were from post or still on-going war ravaged countries; Hungarians, Czechoslovakians and Bulgarians, many with university degrees. There were refugees who had escaped from German concentration camps that had already spent years roaming from camp to camp in Europe. They were true refugees. Many also from Holland and Germany, Italy and Greece, today classified as 'economic' refugees. All of whom were hungry and now in the Promised Land. This Scheyville food hall fed a hungry Europe as never seen before. Some straddled the benches with plates clutched between thighs instead of sitting at the table, so as to be closer to the plate, or perhaps out of fear the food would get stolen. One large Bulgarian man would chew on his mutton chops, pulverising the chop bone with bare teeth. I looked on in amazement. He did it to impress his fellow countrymen, much to their amusement. After the solid food was eaten, one could again tank up or take seconds in the form of a jelly. The jelly was aeroplane jelly. A favourite ad on the radio was, 'I love aeroplane jelly'.

I used to grab slices of bread for afters, and scooped up large quantities of IXL jam available on every table in giant gallon jars. It had huge chunks of real fruit in it. It was lovely, fancy being able to take as much as you liked? Surely Australia so far was everything that it had promised and more! Migrant camps were also the breeding grounds for the budding entrepreneur. Future giants and captains of industry in Australia were often fermented (or fomented, depending on views of capitalism versus socialism) in migrant camps. One Polish man had set up a smart taxi service. He had managed to get one of those large ancient Ford V8 cars and had become a self-proclaimed taxi driver. He knew the way out of the camp having found a route to circumvent the flooded roads. He was doing a good trade, and was helpful in giving information about availability and time tables of the train to Sydney. It would take a few hours, and if leaving early enough one could get back in one day. He would wait for us at the station on the way back from Sydney. We had him drive us to the rail station, which might have been ten or more miles away, and caught the train to Sydney. What followed during our first trip on the train still lives on. The memories growing ever riper and maturing with time. It gets retold every Christmas. But, that will have to wait till next time. Milo, our Jack Russell terrier, is forcing my hand from the keyboard.

Life in Scheyville Camp and My First Bush in 1956.

We soon must move away from Scheyville. Just a few more Scheyville memories that have obsessively stuck through the decades.

After the first few days eating in the communal food hall, we started taking our plates and chops to our own hut. Of course, it was midsummer, and if anything, the food would get even hotter walking outside under the fiery sun.

Some Dutch migrants had, as proof of their lingering culture, obtained bicycles to get around. They would be seen cycling around the camp running messages or getting food. One day, as we were keenly tucking into the mutton in our huts, one of the Dutch cyclers was racing around the huts shouting in Dutch, 'Maggots, maggots in the meat, maggots.' He was like the town crier, all red in the face, too. What was lacking was the bell. It took us a few seconds to reflect upon his message, but soon started to look downwards. Yes, there they were, not too obvious, but when prising open the juicy crevices of the chops, they were there, all wriggling away happily, waiting for their wings. We were eating maggots!

As mentioned earlier, a Pole had become a self-proclaimed taxi-driver. In Holland, this would never be allowed to happen. It was an example of how one could become and have the freedom to initiate an independency without interference from higher up the Australian Bureaucracy. It was a haven of freedom. However, on the way to the train I could hardly look the Polish taxi-driver in the face. I had observed his wife in the shower and seen her 'bush'. The showers were sex separated but in the same block. I had already heard through the camp grapevine that if you took the last cubicle adjacent to the female section one could get a peek. Soon after, I too became privileged to that peek, and had obtained another level of attainment in sexual observations. At that time I was the envy of aspirations held by many boys in their early teens. It was such a specific goal in growing up...I could now hold my head high.

Of course, today those things are observed in all its plucked colonoscopy, chicken wing minutia on the Internet well before fifteen years of age. Different times now, but far more erotic then. It was afterwards and with some guilt (always on automatic), I recognised the woman walking along the mess-hall. I could not look her in the eye. One can imagine going to the Polish taxi-driver's hut when she came out. It was his wife that I had been viewing through the opening of the flimsy shower partition. A deep shame must have coloured me red…But, I was fifteen.

The train trip. We had all settled in the train. Mum was holding a small suitcase in her lap, in which she had packed numerous sandwiches made from the free white bread and previously mentioned free fruit laden IXL jam. Those sandwiches would see us through the day. Frugality would reign in this family through thick and thin but mainly thin. The rhythmic rocking of the train, together with the pleasure of viewing the new passing landscape, was interrupted (never to be forgotten) by the conductor wanting to clip a hole in all the passengers' tickets.

There was something a bit odd about him. He had a dense smell and unfocussed eyes. 'Show us your fickets,' he kept mumbling, swaying along while holding onto Mum's seat. We could not understand what he was saying but knew he might want our tickets. Even so, Dad wanted to know for sure and asked; 'Pardon?' Pronouncing it in French. 'Show us yer fricken thickest mate,' he persevered, now lurching dangerously towards my Mum. She kept her suitcase firmly in her lap. We were by this time getting very alarmed. Were we about to be robbed or worse, was our Mum and her sandwiches at risk? All of a sudden, the conductor gave up all pretence of soberness and just fell on top of Mum and her case with sandwiches. We were all dumb struck. What was this? Someone said, 'He's been on the turps.' We had never heard of this term, didn't know even what 'turps' was. A man who understood our plight gave the hand to mouth gesture indicating drinking. We understood quickly. The passengers helped the man up who stumbled back to his locket. We were so scared. In Holland, we had never observed a drunk. A drunken conductor on a train? What would be waiting for us in Sydney? Luckily, that was the only incident, but it was a great shock to us. We made it back home and the kind Polish taxi driver was waiting at the station. This time I was more brazen and felt that after the shock of the drunken train conductor, a mere peek of his wife in a shower was now an honest well-earned bonus. We had survived some difficult times and I needed something to cheer me up.

So what to make of all this? The few weeks at Scheyville Migrant Camp were totally unexpected. The Nissan huts an extraordinary form of housing that we were totally unprepared for. Not a hint of that during the interview at the Australian Embassy in The Hague. If only there would have been more information right from the beginning. We might still have migrated, but perhaps better prepared. I really thought that our Dutch friends living in Australia would also have given us better information. They had written the most glorious accounts. It was all paved with gold! The isolation of the camp did not really allow us a glimpse of the 'real' Australia. Afterwards, we understood why our friends thought it would be better for us to experience camp life first in order to more appreciate living with them. Was my scepticism of migration 'we did it for the children' born already then? Or, was it a mere dormant incurable curmudgeon gene coming out?

The Magic Car. A Matter of Opinion.

All good things came to an end. We packed up from the Scheyville camp to move in with our Dutch friends who had written to us in Holland about their success in buying their own place within a few years after their arrival in Australia. This sounded like a dream come true. My Mum was especially keen on getting a place with a bathroom. We used to get a coin to visit a public bathhouse in The Hague. The value of the coin would allow a certain time for taking a shower. Of course, we could only afford the shortest of showers with the smallest coin. This meant that one had to undress and shower at the speed of lightning. A very large and always angry man would bang on the door when your time had lapsed.

To have a house with a bathroom was a dream too far in Holland. The glorious letters arriving in Holland from Australia did not take long for Mum to be convinced that our future lay there, where a bathroom could be attained. Dad was more circumspect. However, the colour movie of postmen leaping fences with white-toothed smiling owners on such sunny verdant lawns did impress. His wife could be pretty persuasive. While Mum was the practical partner, Dad was more of the celestial kind. He loved the heavens and stars. Rumour had it that he met my Mum one evening when he walked into a moving tram while staring at the sky. He had a bleeding forehead which she wiped tenderly. They were married within a year. Of course, indulging in star gazing, together with his other passion; short-wave radios, it was difficult to maintain both. Six children running around the table, all shouting, imitating Indians or cowboys. They were trying times during those far too many rainy days in our upstairs apartment.

Mum became even more practical in later life, when she saw her son being interviewed on National TV regarding his recent vasectomy (Helvi was pregnant with number three). Mum reflected, "Oh Helvi, if I had my time over again today, I would have asked dad to do the same." "For sure," she added with gusto. That was a rather big step for Mum, seeing her religion urged all onto, 'Let the little ones come.' Still, it is reassuring that being number two in a line of six, at least I am here to tell the tale

I have no memories of moving into our Dutch friends' house. We would have taken the train to Granville followed by the bus to Woodville Road, Guildford. I do remember Dad asking for the train tickets to Granville but pronouncing it in French. The station master replied, "Wha's dat mate, sayj je it agin"? It took a while but we finally got the tickets. What I do remember also, when walking onto our friends' property, was seeing an old car that had a cabin behind the motor part and a tray behind that. They were the remnants of a utility, or presently known as the 'pick up'. Was this the car that I had fantasized about so much? The half sedan that would morph into a truck by the push of a button? It was indeed. It still had three wheels and a stack of bricks where the fourth one would have been in better times. I never saw it being driven. It might have been 'all that glitters isn't gold', but this old Chevy pick-up sure was past magic.

The house that they had bought --or, what they said they had bought-- was rambling old, but did have a bathroom with a gas geyser at the back in a lean to. It was a bit like the Chevy, had seen better days. It had a rickety but charming veranda with some loose boards and nails sticking out. It faced the sun. On one side it had a few rows of bricks in the shape of a room. In Holland, they had written to us they were planning to put an extra room on so that we would be able to spread out a bit. It must have come to an abrupt end because weeds were growing over the bricks already! We were overjoyed to be away from the camp and the routine of queuing for chops and peas. It was a great opportunity to get our life in order. Dad was to get a job and Mum back to the household routine. She had her washing machine shipped over from Holland. We were grateful and happy for a number of days. It wasn't till my Dad found out he would not be able to get a job within the Government that things turned a bit bleak again. Non-British subjects (together with non-whites) were barred from

Governmental jobs. He went to bed not to get up for another six weeks. Fortunately, I did get a job with a special ticket of dispensation from the Government, allowing me to work even though I was still under age. I loved earning money from the first time I received my pay packet. It was real cash in a beige envelope with my name and number of hours worked. It even contained paper money. I kept counting it out over and over again.

The German shepherd With Three Legs and Cake Eating.

The Dutch Friends' house, as previously mentioned, was old, and must have been a farm house before the arrival of thousands of immigrants pushing further and further inland. Hill after hill were conquered with houses replacing trees and grazing cows. The sound of hammers, machinery and coarse oaths renting the grey blue smoky air. It was an era of every migrant's dream of achieving your own home on your own solid block of land come true. This old farm house was now the missing tooth amidst the sea of many a migrant's suburban prosperity. In fact, the old house was now in the middle of a huge timber and building material yard supplying the frenetic race for building houses. Large stacks of different sized timber were balanced precariously hither and dither amongst stacks of baths, concrete laundry basins and other building materials. All this surrounded by a grey muddy clay that made getting to the house a slippery event. Bricks were placed here and there, enabling one to hop from one to the other without risking wet feet or slipping down all together. No doubt my parents could have experienced a less grim and more cheerful beginning, but that's how it was. Perhaps many might well have thought it a very cheerful beginning. However, our pioneering spirit was a bit lukewarm and run-down after Scheyville migrant camp and maggots meals.

The timber yard was protected by a large German shepherd. It was a very friendly and compassionate animal, forever greeting those who entered the yard, foe or friend. It also had three legs. One of its hind legs was missing, in tandem with the old Chevy. He did not so much guard the timber yard from thieves as he did chase rats that used to do Ring-a-Ring-a-Rosie between the stacks of timber, scurrying like a flash when he arrived. The rats would scatter each time a crane moved a stack of timber, then quickly scurry under the next lot of beams. The dog did his best but rats are clever and soon knew they had it over the dog. They used to dart out in full view, taunting him, only to quickly hide whenever he lifted his head. It was amusing to watch. There was a king rat almost the size of a cat who asserted himself over his tribe. They would only follow if he made the first move. They would move in a specific, strictly disciplined and regimented order in a V-shape behind the undisputed king-rat. No rat would come inside the house because of two very large cats holding sentry near the entrances. The cats had all their legs intact, which was something for us to cling to.

Whenever my Dad could rouse himself from bed he would observe from the sunny veranda, the bustle of cranes, trucks and the scuffles between the dog, cats and rats. We knew things were improving with Dad when Mum caught him one night looking at the sky through a pair of binoculars. He had found the Milky Way! A kind of peace came over him after his discovery of this Southern hemisphere's heavenly night-sky. (My Dad was always a keen observer of the celestial world. Much more than the real world.) My job was progressing from cleaning the factory floor and getting the workers' lunches to being initiated to use the machinery. The lunches for workers was the first sign of Australia being 'paved with gold', when apple-pies, Big Ben meat pies and bottles of Fanta were ordered as if it was normal. It was normal! Can you imagine? What we would look forward to once a year back in Holland on a birthday, was the daily norm here. Not only the norm. As proof of absolute opulence and belching richness, parts of the pies would be slung onto the floor as if it was nothing. I had the job of cleaning those carelessly flung out morsels, still warm and oozing. I was almost on my knees in admiration of a country so endowed with the splendour of excess. I wrote earlier about the amazing antics of workers in factories whereby the proverb 'Australia, where men are men but the sheep are nervous,' had more than a tinge of truth to it. Perhaps with the sexes being so far apart and the not so distant years of convicts and penal camps it was no surprise that this cultural phenomenon had survived and was still being played out between factory workers. I did not join this dating, and as a foreigner and migrant was somehow spared from these antics. The owner of the factory had a creaking leg and you always knew he was coming. I never asked, and no one ever told me, but I suppose he had lost a leg during the last war. Why was it that during those first few months things were missing, first the magic Chevy wheel, then the German shepherd dog's leg, and now a factory owner with just one leg?

My weekly wages I gave to my Mum, but I was to keep money earned by overtime. I had a small steel box in which I would put my savings. The more overtime, the more would be deposited in this small safe. The safe could be locked and I kept the key. Overtime was paid time and a half, and on Saturdays time and a half for morning and double after twelve o'clock, with Sundays always double time. It was a time of enormous power by unions, and bosses had to comply or else! As the weeks went by, Dad finally roused himself and managed to get a job as well. He donned overalls and steel capped boots. We were on our way!

Our Dutch friends' only son had managed to buy a very small Renault in which the family would all pile in on a Sunday for church on top of the hill. The car was very small, more like a jacket really. They sat in each other's laps, and when hurtling down home after the service would burst out and spread on the sunny veranda. The wife (aunty) made a large pot of coffee and all would delve into eating big cake. This part of their accounts to us in Holland was absolutely true. The cake would be there each Sunday and it was clear they all enjoyed it. Australia at its best.

Cake eating each Sunday was factual and true. What was not true was that they had bought the old house! It was rented. The row of bricks that was supposed to be an extra room was abruptly halted when the owner of the timber yard and old house asked what the plan was. He did not want space taken up where he could put his building materials. He was a successful migrant himself.

One Cannot Live Of Disillusionment Alone.

With a magic car on three wheels, a dog on three legs, many normal rats on all fours, but against that a factory owner with a creaking wooden leg, it was time for our family to bring some normalcy about. With Dad's discovery of the Southern night's sky and his beloved study of the Milky Way restored, things were on the upper trajectory once again. I was earning money, and so was my brother, Frank. Even Dad now donned a blue Yakka overall and put shoulders under the task of pitching in towards a better future. The premise of 'we do it for the children' had to be fulfilled. No good regretting and mulling over what was. Past is past, and Holland is cold now, and probably raining as well.

In those days, jobs were everywhere, and I managed to learn a lot on all sorts of heavy engineering machinery. The lathe, heavy presses and milling machines seemed to be everywhere I went. Piece work was introduced as an incentive for workers to earn more than just a wage. Of course, the shields to protect workers from getting limbs cut off were often disabled to save time in cutting or pressing and milling the next bit of bolt or drilled bracket. I noticed hands with missing fingers. With piece work and overtime I just about doubled my weekly earnings and my metal box was singing its praise with all those savings tucked inside. I wasn't too stingy, though, and allowed myself a packet of ten Craven A's cigarettes and the occasional Fanta orange drink with pie. A glorious celebratory gesture towards this golden paved Australia.

Mum decided that we needed to get away to our own accommodation as quickly as possible. Our Dutch friends gave us the opportunity to achieve this by asking very little in rent, or perhaps none at all. I can't remember. I do remember that the place they lived in was not theirs but belonged to the timber yard owner. A bit of confusion, but 'owning' our own house was a concept we had no real understanding of anyway. That was yet to come! Apart from overtime earnings, all our income was pooled and given to Mum to try and move away to a better place. We sought to move away from the piles of timber with dust and mud. One of the daughters taught me the basics of photo developing which we did in the back lean-to. It was also the bathroom with the hot gas geyser above it. There was nothing like the hot weekly bath to luxuriate in at the end of a sixty hour work week.

I also remember thinking of Anna Magnani of 'The Rose Tattoo', that I had seen during those culturally lean times. As I was taking this hot bath I noticed the Van

Dijk's daughter, Lisbeth, walking by outside. She looked at me inside through the window. I was in the bath with Anna Magnani keeping me spiritual company. It might have been a case of being curious about the nude male. There might also have been a healthy awakening of her hormones. She was about twelve or thirteen. In any case, she had a quick look, but from the angle of her eyes she observed more than just my face. During the six months or so that we lived with the Dutch friends, the rather pleasant memory involving the bathroom with Lisbeth looking in wasn't all there was to it. On Sundays, it was the norm still to dress up in Sunday best. My pants would be pressed, and its crease would be preserved as much as possible, at least during the morning. I would hitch up the crease when crossing legs, and so did my Dad and other brothers wearing long pants, at least till coffee and cakes had been consumed. With the ironed pants came a nice blue shirt and tie fastened by a clasp to be perfectly centred at all times. On top of that a sports jacket, but this would be kept off during the Sunday cake eating. When cake eating was finished, Lisbeth and I wandered off to the next allotment behind the house that was somewhat secluded from views with stacks of baths (my Mum's dream) and some bushes. I have forgotten on the why and how, but suddenly Lisbeth grabbed my tie clasp and ran away with it. I gave chase and caught her quickly. She laughed but I remained serious. It was my tie clasp. I tried to take it back but she would not give in, and kept it firmly in her grip while tucking both hands between her legs. I wrestled, but was too religious or shy to act deliberately inappropriately by grabbing her between her legs and hands to retrieve my tie clasp. I instead went to safer grounds and put one of my hands upwards on her tiny breasts, knowing full well that the clasp would not be found there. It was a moment of daring, and my second exploration of the female softness. Keen readers would remember a previous attempt less than a year before when still in Holland. There was a shout from the house. One of the sisters who taught me the photo developing thought it had gone far enough. She was hanging from the top window and called us back home. And that was that. I never got my tie clasp back. They were lean times in exploring the sexual awakenings of my youth. My Mum always taught me to make the best of things. 'Gerard,' she often said, 'you have to row with oars that you were given.' So true.

Moving Onto 'Our Own' Block of Land with 'Deposit' & 'Easy Terms.'

Leaving the lean times and memories of tie-clips and perky breasts (furtively enjoyed in the timber yard) behind, we will now go forward to an episode that too might have been significant in my opinion of migration, and the persistent scepticism of it. That is not to say that had we remained living in Holland things would have turned out any different. To now have reached a level of freedom, hopefully some insight, and to have the luxury of enough time still left to come up with some answers regarding migration scepticism has always been my aim.

The saving for the future was now on in earnest. My Mum became the financial wizard and accountant. It had to be struck with a compromise between pocket money and fast saving to get our own place to live. How we slept those first few months I have no memory. We had nothing on arrival except the clothes we wore, and the four steel trunks that travelled with us on the boat. The vacuum cleaner, and the pride of our street back in The Hague, was the electric washing machine which we had shipped over separately. We could wash our clothes and vacuum, but on what did we sleep? I can't remember anything about bedding. Did we sleep upright? It is possible, but I don't think so. Migrants are made of pioneering stuff, but upright sleeping was never an option. Right now, people would probably reflect and call migrating seeking a life-style! We surely would have bought some sort of bedding as a priority.

Our own Block with garage (temporary Dwelling.) Little brother tending a cabbage.

The extra hours worked above the normal forty became vital. Each day, Mum would wait for us to come home, but it was always welcomed if we came home later than expected. 'Overtime,' at time-and-a-half would bring our aim of moving into own place closer and closer. Of course, work on Saturday or Sunday was as close to heaven as Dad's Milky Way. Double-time money delirium! Even though it meant forgoing the cake eating event on the creaky veranda during the Sunday morning. Our very religious Mum thought the foregoing of compulsory church going just a minor sin. Dad would put his pay packet under Mum's dinner plate each pay day, which I think was on a Thursday. Dad did this as a kind of weekly joke, as if tipping the waitress for a nice meal. It might read a bit strange, but families have their own jokes, don't they? I would just give my earnings to Mum straight away without any formalities or any joking, and so did my elder brother, Frank. The coffer was swelling, slowly at first, but with increasing speed in tandem with the urgency.

One of the items still to be told to complete a picture of our stay with the Dutch friends and their generosity of allowing us to get on our own feet, was the early morning urinating rituals. The old house at the time we were living in it was crowded with two large families. The Dutch family with five children and ours with six, making a total of fifteen, including both sets of parents. The toilet was outside and at the back of the lean-to that I used as a dark room, and for all of us a bathroom. It was quite a walk, often too far for us, and the boys would share their number one's with the rats and three-legged dog against the stacks of timber outside. This was especially so at waking times. There was a flimsy partition between our portion of the house and that of our friends who had the larger part, including a couple of bedrooms upstairs. The four girls sleeping upstairs would run down each morning and urinate loudly in a bucket which was next to the flimsy partition and clearly audible. This would result in a loud Dutch howl of laughter and coarseness from me and my brothers on the other side of the partition. We almost woke up early not to miss the ritual. That's how it was then!

Over the next six months, we heard amongst other Dutch migrants that the way forward was to get your own block of land with a garage on it. The available time left after working over-time was taken up by endless discussions on our own block of land. It sounded like something out of Steinbeck's, 'Of Mice and Men'. And it was far above my Dad's understanding or his interests, but not my Mum. She knew the way forward was to do what other people advised us about. It wasn't just the talk of other migrants. The world of 'real estate' seemed to be everywhere, and Australia was at the fore-front of owning a block of land and better still, a block of land with a house on it. It was the very essence of what success was about. In any case, renting was a waste of money and everyone nodded in agreement. It wasn't made clear why that was so. But questioning ownership wasn't on the horizon of pioneering migrants. Renting is what they had left behind!

It was a contagion that still lives on today. Nothing eases awkward social occasions better than the mentioning of 'real estate' and 'home ownership' around the dining table, or even standing around an art gallery sipping the chardonnay while discussing Edvard Munch's, 'The Scream'. Mum understood the language of 'own block near railway station', of mortgages, easy terms, deposits and interest rates immediately, and had worked out that with the present level of income from Dad and her two eldest sons, including so much over-time, we already had a 'deposit' for own block. Deposit and own block had the Oosterman family firmly in its grip. They were holy. My Dad remained puzzled why we could not just go to the local council and ask to be provided with a modest home to live in. It was now all so different.

After a while, he was happy with the star-lit heavens and totally trusted his wife to steer us into the security of our own block and garage. The garage was allowed to be lived in as long as its door was painted the same as the walls. Better still, take the garage door off and replace with a window to then help the local council to simply designate the garage into 'a temporary dwelling'. It sounded so much more domestic than garage, and was legal to boot.

Those First Two Years of Hard Yakka.

The garage was eight by four metres.

The move from the old house to our own block of land with garage (Temporary Dwelling) was achieved after much searching by my Mum scanning the 'Blocks of

Land" for sale in newspapers. Enough money had been saved. And even though my Mum's English was very poor, that was no hindrance. She would just speak Dutch with a few English sounding vowels thrown in. Through weekend meetings with other migrants, the fever of achieving this first goal had bedded down. Inquiries of deposits and how getting a loan was made 'easy' by building societies, was now well understood by our Mum. Estate agents would drive her around to the different blocks for sale and her appraisal. She would be quick to measure the distance to the nearest railway station and distance from the city. The closest to city and station, the more desirable, and also more costly. Sydney was spread out over an area almost the size of Holland, and with everyone feverishly seeking their own house on their own block, it doesn't take a genius to understand why suburbia reigns in Australian cities like nowhere else. Ownership of a car then becomes as essential as sleeping on a mattress. Selling blocks of land and cars was a main ingredient and driving force for a future prosperous Australia. It still is.

We were totally swept into having to buy/build our house after arriving in Australia. To be able for most to achieve this, housing was made from as cheap a material as possible, hence the thin sheeting to clad the houses both inside and outside, making them not much more than windbreaks. The asbestos cement sheeting was at the forefront of those cheap building materials. It had -- and still has-- dire consequences. In Australia, there are hundreds of thousands of ageing homes clad with that material.

The day of moving into our first dwelling is still etched into my mind like nothing else (apart from my first juvenile experiences of 'female bush and breasts'). All our belongings were piled on a truck with a driver. They must have been hired for the day. It was much more than we thought. The four steel trunks, all our bedding and washing machine, the ice box and six children's clothes and bits and pieces that we had acquired during the six months we lived with our Dutch friends. All were piled on the truck, including Dad, who had to try and prevent our belongings from getting blown off during the trip to our new place. He was spreadeagled on top of the truck with arms and legs flailing, trying to keep all on the truck. The truck drove off and I can still see my Dad thrashing about on his back.

This photo was taken after moving in to our own first home, the asbestos-lined garage or Temporary Dwelling! Brother John (deceased) at front, Mum and Dad with glasses together (single bed), my sister Dora on floor, smiling Frank on top right and Herman and Adrian on left top and bottom right. The mattress at front was vacant as I was taking the picture.

We moved in and Mum and Dad must have been busy to prepare all the bedding. Us kids were so proud and we would walk backwards and forwards over the own block of land like eighteenth century aristocrats inspecting a newly inherited tract of land in Bavaria. There were no more rats, no three-legged dogs. We were on our own. Dad had even survived the trip sprawled out on the back of the truck.

The Throwing Of a Geographical Dart in Sydney.

While the distance to rail-station and shops were all important, as well as owning own block with having a temporary dwelling (garage) for living in, the social aspects of a particular area were totally unknown. I don't think this was at all considered. It was all to do with practical objectives and affordability. Comparisons with other Dutch migrants generally were about price, distance from infrastructure, and size of our own block. Driving around, it all looked rather the same with well-kept lawns and nodding petunias being prominent. Liking or disliking a certain area because of a 'milieu', or making a choice between any social and cultural differences, if any, did not feature between migrated people. They were lucky enough to have at least made it to getting a place to move into. No matter how humble or culturally isolated it might be.

Within a few weeks after moving into our own garage, a lean to was built between our garage and the next door fence. This increased the liveable space by fifty percent. A huge difference. The corrugated asbestos sheeting had not been pushed under the existing roof sheeting far enough. Each time it rained heavily the water would bank up and run back and into the lean to and above the bunks. Herman and I slept on the lower beds, but John and Frank were not so lucky. Dad, who wasn't very handy, had pinned plastic sheeting above the bunks and underneath the corrugated roof sheeting against the wooden rafters. He was hoping the water would just run down the inside of the plastic sheeting. He hoped against the odds, that the water would flow outside again between the gap of the fibro wall sheets and the bottom timber plate. However, the slope of the roof and plastic sheeting wasn't acute or steep enough, and water would well up in frighteningly large bubbles, inches above the peacefully sleeping bodies. In winter, with the outside just four millimetres away, it wasn't very nice when this bubble would spill and flood the unsuspected sleepers. Of course, during daytime rain, Mum would relieve the water bubble by pushing it upwards and out. In time, we all took responsibility by waking in turns to relieve this water flood emergency above the two bunks. During heavy rain I could not be bothered to try and sleep, knowing my turn would soon arrive so just sat in a chair all night, watching the water bubbles swell up and then relieve the threat, giving the others a reasonable sleep. It was a good time for melancholia to thrive and ponder reflections of past and possible futures.

If you look at the previous article photo where we are all in beds and on the floor you might have noticed a curtain. This curtain would be drawn with all the floor mattresses tucked in between the beds at the back of the garage and out of sight. This would then create a small lounge-dining-kitchen area. At night, four boys slept in the lean-to which also kept the trunks with our clothing. At the other end of the garage, opposite my parents' bedding (and Dora and Adrian's), there was a small electric stove with one hot-plate, and underneath a minuscule oven. My Mum cooked the most amazing meals on this miniature electric stove/oven. We were always hungry. Above this little stove was the electric hot water for the trickle shower. Next to the sink was the shower cubicle. My Dad had jammed a round stick between the rickety shower walls to hold up a plastic shower sheet strung from plastic rings. It wasn't unusual for someone to take a shower while Mum was working above the stove creating a magic meal, only for the shower curtain to collapse spontaneously. This would be met with howls of laughter from all of us, but not the hapless victim standing naked just a metre or so away from our steaming meal. In the evenings, the boys had to do home-work, but as a reward would listen to a radio play, 'The Adventures of Smokey Dawson'. They were the events of the week over the whole of Australia syndicated across more than a hundred radio stations. Isn't it amazing how we were spellbound by voices telling a story over the radio?

We met the neighbours within a few weeks. Again it was our Mum who made the move. She was fearless, and despite speaking mainly in Dutch, she would knock on the door. It has to be remembered that houses in Australia are rather private. The whole street's housing was uniformly barred from the inside and outside by sternly refusing anyone to get an inkling of what might be going on inside. Not a movement would ever escape to the outside. At night, one could sometimes detect a sliver of faint light escaping through obstinate Venetian blinds, double backed up by layers of white lacy material, and for extra security and more darkness, heavy curtains. Dad wondered why they bothered with windows. It wasn't easy to break through, but our Mum wasn't to be deterred. She made friends. Years later, after my parents moved back for good to Holland and were on a trip back to Australia and their former home, the neighbours organised a surprise party for them. They remembered her efforts in bringing not only the neighbours together, but also that some would now live with open curtains and have proper sit-downs with cups of tea.

She made a difference.

Frank and Our Own House.

Life in the garage with Mum looking on. My Lambretta scooter with my sister Dora.

This shot was taken just before my trip to Melbourne through the Snowy Mountains on my Lambretta scooter. It would be a trip of well over two thousand kilometres. I packed enough clothing, a small tent and some cooking utensils, including, I suppose, a fork and knife. I went with a Dutch friend who had a Vespa. The Vespa was considered a bit more upmarket. During that period I became part of a scooter club that met fortnightly at an ambulance-hall in Parramatta. My friend took a complete suit with him. He knew a girl from our migrant boat who lived near Melbourne! He planned to visit her. I did not know any girls, but was keen on them, even from a distance.

The trouble with Frank might well have been one reason for this trip. I wanted to get away! It was such a creeping illness. The behaviour did not add up, and it must have been such a puzzle. Why would Frank so often behave bizarre? He was his own worst enemy, and even though at times he was sorry for his behaviour, it would not stop. He seemed incapable of stopping. My parents hoped that with the move into a bigger house, things would get better. We were counselled by my Mum to try and accept Frank and include him more. However, all of us were younger than Frank. We might have felt sorry, I did, but we also had our own friends and growing up to do. Slowly, Frank did become excluded.

It was all too strange and upsetting. I would hear my parents talking into the deep of the night about the problem of Frank. It crept into our lives like nothing else. Not even the experiences of migration and the sardine like condition in our previous fibro garage came close to this problem. Let alone understanding the reasons or getting it resolved. It was all getting dark, and the joy of living in our own house was slowly leaching away. It could be tempting to feel that the migration and other traumas affected Frank badly, but there were already things with Frank before the immigration from Holland. I remember Frank was taken out of high-school in Holland to learn a trade with a watchmaker. However, it did not last long...Frank's behaviour already then was becoming erratic. He would be obsessive about certain things and not with other more important issues. He was becoming a bit outside of things.

After Frank's run with so many jobs in Australia, almost on a weekly basis, it must have dawned on my parents that Frank had a serious problem. It all came to a head when, once again, Frank became violent. In a fit of inexplicable anger he threw a pair of scissors at our brother, John. The scissors were sticking out of John's thigh. My Dad took the pointy scissors out while Frank escaped through the front door. At the time, Dad was doing some drying of dishes. Dad followed Frank outside with the dish towel still hanging over his shoulder. Frank was faster, with Dad in pursuit. Frank, half way up the hill, then ran into someone's garden and hid himself between the azaleas. As Dad arrived, with tea towel still slung over his shoulder, the owner of the house and garden came out brandishing a shot gun. Without mucking about, further ado, or contemplation of this strange event with Frank hiding in his azaleas, the man pointed his gun at the sky and fired a deafening shot. This seemed to calm the situation. The police arrived and Frank was taken away. This was the last day in Frank's life where he would enjoy a normal family life. Of course, 'normal family life' is open to question and has endless variations. Nothing is really normal. So much still to come and so many answers go begging.

Frank and Callan Park Asylum.

The firing of the shotgun and the commotion in the street resulted with Frank being put in a police paddy wagon. My parents were interviewed. They must have told police of problems they were having with Frank's violence. The incident with the scissors was considered serious enough and culminated with Frank being taken away to Callan Park for assessment. Callan Park was a mental asylum situated close to the City in very large park like surroundings. It consisted of many double story Georgian old sandstone buildings. It had a very high wall around it and looked intimidating when approached from the front. It would be Frank's main home for the next fourteen years. He was diagnosed as suffering from schizophrenia.

A sigh of relief was washing over our family. The children came home from school without fear and expectation of another shemozzle or explosion of anger. We could sit around without skulking away in our rooms, out of troubles' way. Dad and Mum were happy that Frank would now get care and attention from experts in a place designed for people with a mental illness. A cure or some form of action would be initiated, and Frank would get back in charge of a life and return home soon. That must have been my parents' fervent wish. And surely not one that could be seen as extravagant?

It has to be admitted that my view of Australia hasn't always been so benign and lofty. I have spent far more years here than anywhere else and am a naturalised Australian, born in Holland. So why, at times, the chagrin? The naturalisation ceremony and oath were taken with swearing allegiance to the Queen of England, which I thought odd as I could have sworn we migrated to Australia. But, the cup-o-tea and the S.A.O. (Salvation Army Officer) crackers with 'tasty' cheese afterwards were welcome. It was a mass naturalisation ceremony at the Sydney Town Hall. It was a period when cinema goers were slowly starting to refuse to stand up for the National Flag raising and Save the Queen anthem before the movie. Some cinemas had a Hammond organ rising up majestically from below the stage. A Liberace-like suited and war medalled bedecked man would belt out this Anthem. It did not help, and soon no one stood up anymore, and this little irrelevant ditty was dropped. Oddly enough, Australia today still prefers the monarchy to a republic.

We could not get over our first visit to Frank in that hospital/asylum. The sun wasn't shining much better with Frank not at home. The nightmare of Callan Park courtyard, with bunches of keys hanging from the scowling wardens belts, wasn't acceptable, nor the wrapping up of Frank in wet bed-sheets when he became violent. This was 1960 not 1860. Frank soon came home again.

Wedding photo of my parents with Mum's brother and sister.

Art and Burgeoning Business Acumen.

After Frank came home again, we all went straight back to fear and anticipation of more outbursts. My Dad did have contact with some doctors at Callan Park. If we wanted Frank to stay there if he wasn't well, there was a procedure whereby he could be admitted as an involuntary patient of the asylum permanently. It also meant he would not and could not come home, even for visits. It seemed a very strange law but there was no way out if we wanted Frank to not come home when he wasn't well. He would be there at the 'pleasure' of the Government. It seemed a very draconian way. Surely, Frank's freedom would be curtailed, and from what we had seen of Callan Park, it was an asylum straight out of Bedlam. Many of the patients seemed like caged animals, walking up and down automatically. I remember my aunt taking me to a zoo as a child and seeing a tiger in a small cage just walking up and down, up and down. Many patients were deeply institutionalised. In fact, the asylum worked as a de-facto jail. Today, jails are used as de-facto mental hospitals.

We wanted Frank to come home when he was well and not when he wasn't, in which case we could visit him. We thought that enough care at Callan Park would ensure he would not travel home when he wasn't well enough. That seemed impossible to achieve. Officialdom and obstinate entrenched bureaucracy was the essence of Anglo culture with the 'don't change if it isn't broke' reigning high at all levels, even today. This is in direct contrast to the Dutch 'if it isn't broke, break it and start anew, try and improve!' My parents would never allow the permanent involuntary locking up of their son in an institute.

The one item missing in Frank's life at Callan Park was genuine care. He used to get the train back home with his family in a dreadful state. My parents could not understand how a person obviously unwell could just wander in and out of the hospital. It seemed there was just no supervision. The answer by the authorities was for Frank to be 'scheduled'. The explanation of that type of hospitalisation or care, was for Frank to be locked up in an institute. The contemplation of that was too horrifying. There did not seem to be anything that would suit Frank. It was all so grimly black and white. No subtleties or something in between. Why would any patient be allowed to wander the streets? It seemed incomprehensible. When Frank started to arrive home clad in his pyjamas that my parents knew that something had to be done. Home life became dreadful, and all would scatter when Frank arrived in an unwell state. Dad and I developed an antenna that would transmit signals when Frank was about to become unwell. Mum did not have such an antenna. She would fuss and exhort Frank to brush his hair, clean the room, and tidy up or this or that. It clearly irritated him. We would tell her to just leave him be, but Mum never picked up on that. She wanted Frank to accept her love and care. Schizophrenia does not adhere to giving normal responses.

It is such a baffling disease and experience. Frank would know he had misbehaved and wanted to be taken back to Callan Park. He felt genuinely contrite. Poor Frank.

At my sister's or brother's wedding (I have forgotten), we were all standing in front of the church steps. The steps ran up to the church entrance. There might have been forty or more people including Frank standing on the back step behind the groom and bride, all looking radiant. The photographer was almost ready to take the obligatory wedding photos, and when we had all synchronised our positions and smiles, Frank all of a sudden pushed our brother, Herman, down the steps. It was always on the cards, and I had warned Mum not to have Frank at the wedding.

Frank came to me and asked to be taken back to Callan Park. 'Just put me on the train', he said. He always felt remorse afterwards, yet could not prevent his outbursts. I took him to the train back to Callan Park. Some years later, I gave Frank a job working on a building side doing painting. He did well for a few days, including singing his favourite song, 'Singin in the Rain'. The Greek painters thought he was hilarious. 'You have a funny brother', they told me. During one lunch while sitting on a ledge which had a steep drop to one side when Frank took a swipe at me. I told Frank that that could not be done on the job. He said, 'I know, Gerard, take me back to Callan Park.' We walked back to his second home, Callan Park, and we said goodbye.

I have written before about Callan Park. There was a royal commission in 1961, and as Royal commissions go, a bit of an exoneration for all from the private school boys clubs that generally manoeuvre themselves into lucrative Royal Commissions. Many years later, another Royal Commission on the Private Hospital Chelmsford's deep sleep therapy was undertaken. It was found that many patients had died while under the care of Dr Harry

Baily. He committed suicide after the investigation on the deaths of many patients. Dr Harry Baily was the superintendent at Callan Park when Frank was admitted. Some years before, and married to the lovely Helvi, I was phoned by my Mum to drive quickly to Callan Park. 'Your Dad is on his way to try and kill Dr Harry Bailey.' After Helvi and I arrived, we noticed my Dad hopping mad, running through the rhododendrons at Callan Park. It was in the nick of time. Hot murder in his eyes. Poor Dad, driven to the very edge of his sanity, as well.

I now will try and get to happier words. While all this was happening, I did a course in creative drawing together with a certificate in quantity surveying. I still don't know or understand why I did the latter. A complete mystery, a blank each time I mull over that strange choice. I had worked at several jobs and knew how to save. One of those jobs was painting, and I understood how to try and get my own contracting business going. Maybe the strange course was an idea to break into the world of contracting. In any case, I knew how to price jobs, from bills of quantities submitted on my requests from architects and builders. I had letterheads printed with matching envelopes, always a good impression beating others who would scribble their quotes on bits of paper. I soon had a good and lucrative contracting business. I made good money. I also did swinging stage work on the outside of buildings. I had no fear of heights, either. Another lucky break.

The Ford V8 Period and Other Stuff.

The next shot I found yesterday in a box full of photos. It is very interesting, and shows perfectly our situation at that time. My Dad seems to be sitting on an asbestos sheet wearing a tie and utter resignation. Frank, shirtless at the front. My sister Dora cuddling our pet dog, Mum in a deck chair. I seem to be just hanging on. The plight of our lives seems so clear. The house behind Dad on the other side of the road does have windows, but although Venetian blinds were at pitch fever popularity, so was 'privacy'. England had moats and drawbridges, Australia had blinds. The house next to the venetians had a Dutch family living in it. They had open doors and windows.

Seeping despair in the New Country

As I motor-biked past a car sales yard, I noticed a large car for sale amongst many others. This car was a powder blue colour. Its chrome glimmered seductively. They say men fall in love with cars. Even the primates shown recently on TV, the male gets drawn to anything with wheels while the female ape cuddles dolls. What hope have we got? As a male homo sapien, men might as well do away with free choice when a car sales yard beckons us more than a bevy of dolls. I mean, what could be nicer than cuddling a doll? Yet, it is the hot embrace of high revving steel pistons and killer speeds that men seem to be drawn to. The smarmy salesman saw me coming, looking out from his little window inside his pigeon-hole office overlooking his domain of gaping cars. The perfect customer. A young man on the hunt for his first car.

'Care to take a closer look?' the man said, while consolidating his opinion of me. He had seen so many come and go that day but not many young ones. He could spot an easy sale, having honed his car salesmanship at his previous sales yard along Parramatta Road called 'Pacific Cars Is Terrific'. He had broken the back of many a customer's reluctance. He knew the ropes and his cars, and was keenly sought after around the car-yard precincts of Sydney. The year would have been around 1961/62. I had gone through a Lambretta scooter, then I bought an ex-police bike with side-car which I used to go rabbit and fox hunting with my brother, John. John was very tall, over two metres. I don't know how we fitted a tent, two rifles and big John in the outfit, but we must have. When one is young, matters of comfort are hardly ever considered. When getting to my present age, comfort is all, and sleeping in a tent gets a bit hazardous with serpents and crocodiles around, not to mention huge poisonous cane toads that can kill by leaving a slimy substance. After seventy, the inner spring mattress beckons like a nun waiting for her habit.

I walked around this blue car, both clock-wise and anti. The tension between us was palpable. I knew what it felt like to drive a bunch of two wheeled condensed steel, wherever I steered it to, but also felt that to be inside a car was going to be a different experience. The salesman remained quiet so far, confident his prey was now slowly being seduced. 'They all get to it, sooner or later,' he surmised philosophically. 'Would you like to go inside, get the feel of it?' Of course I would. No sooner the door was opened, I slid inside. Leather seats, a cigarette lighter! The salesman nonchalantly stalked back to his office. The perfect ploy. He knew his trade so well. The master at work.

As soon as I sat inside the car, I was gone. The smooth feel of the steering wheel, and the smell of waxed leather. It had a huge back seat as well, with inbuilt ash trays. I could drive my parents around. A real treat for the family. I got out and went to the office. The salesman put the phone down. 'I want to buy the car,' I said. 'Oh, I just had an enquiry about the same car, a bloke had a look earlier on,' the salesman said with cruel intent. I signed the papers with two years of payments on 'easy terms,' and drove off. The car, a Ford Single spinner V8 cost two hundred and twenty pounds. Oh, what a feeling!

Mum with (late) brother John's wife Jenny behind her. Helvi looking at camera, then my brother Herman, brother-in-law Dieter, and my sister Dora. Notice, we are sitting on paint drums! The Broadway slow combustion wood-heater. A real Christmas tree and candles. They were very good and happy times.

The Learning of the Fox Trot and More V8 Memories.

Of course, with the powder-blue Ford V8 sedan, and the family being treated to a few tours around Sydney, my thoughts went to try and get to know more about the opposite sex. These were lean times spent with females. Harking back to the Scheyville migrant camp with the very limited and lonely Polish pubic bush peek through the shower partition, the experience had exhausted itself. I decided to take the bull by the horn, and take some dancing lessons. I noticed that in some magazines of the type, 'boy wants to meet girl' kind, or the reverse, photos of the boys were often taken while nonchalantly leaning with one foot elevated into the door- way of a car. A photo leaning one-footed in the sidecar of my motor bike wasn't all that exciting a prospect for a girl to be taken out in. I mean, on A Roman Holiday the girls rode around on a Vespa. That was a bit different from driving around the mute and deadly quiet streets of suburban Sydney, and its sleeping petunias, in an ex-police motor bike. Even with a sidecar.

The nous for someone with a guttural accent to get to know a girl in a strange country might now have to include a photo of myself leaning casually in my Ford V8. Even then, I feared it might just not melt the tigers enough to make the butter. I needed some flair, more oomph, and perhaps some chutzpah. Before placing an ad in a lonely heart's magazine I decided to take dancing lessons from Phyllis Bates dancing academy. I had already learnt that the word 'academy' was used in Australia with careless abandon. I mean, that word in Holland meant professors and Leiden University, or an eight year ballet course in Russia's Moscow's Bolshoi. Here, an 'academy' could be doing Jiu jitsu, car repairs, or jigging about above a Greek milk bar. In any case, this dancing academy offered a booklet of twenty tickets on 'special'. In the late fifties and sixties, everything was 'special'. Even a locally built car was named General Motor's 'Holden special.' You did not have much that was sold 'not special.' The one thing that remained static and fixed, even till now, is that some cheese surviving today, is still sold as 'tasty.'

The flooding of the love-market was heavily tilted towards single bull necked males with strong gnarled horned hands. They were the ones to build the Snowy Mountain's Electricity supply scheme, now redundant; the digging of mines at MT Isa, now redundant; the manual cutting of sugar cane in hot Queensland, now by giant machines. I thought that by learning to do a nifty fox-trot or even a quick-step, I would have an edge over the Queensland cane-cutters and bulky Bulgarians when it came to getting to know a girl with a lovely smile. I duly took the train to Sydney after donning a clean Pelaco shirt, finely ironed by my Mum, and a smart Reuben-Scarf suit (two for the price of one). I walked to Pitt Street and clambered the stairs up to Phyllis Bates Academy (above the milk bar), and presented my booklet of twenty tickets. After a ticket was ripped out of my booklet, I entered a room where I could hear a lively tune being played. A very nice cone-shaped bra-encased woman came to me, and after introduction told me she would start to teach me a fox trot.

'Just follow the painted footsteps on the floor,' and, 'I'll guide you.' Just start, one two...one two. I hopped along, but could hardly believe a woman was holding me. I mean a real woman! To think I still had nineteen tickets left. I could hardly contain my pleasure, but did notice that most of the dance students were all bulky cane cutter Bulgarian males. The teacher in the meantime said, 'You have to hold me in such a way that a book must be firmly held between us, and not fall on the floor.' The last thing I wanted for future memories was the misery of being unable to even hold the book between me and a female body, and suffer the ignominy of a failed book holder while learning the fox trot.

But, where are the girls? So much yet to come.

Vic's Cabaret and First Date.

With the Phyllis Bates 'academy' dance lessons firmly tucked under my arms, I was ready and willing to go, and practise for the first time my dancing without the pre-painted dance-steps on a floor. An Austrian Waltz was the last one I was taught. At one stage I came close to losing the book held between us. I had to place my leg (just one) between both the lovely teacher's legs, and do a majestic sweep of a one hundred eighty degree turn while holding my chin proudly upwards and sideways. I had at the same time to hold both my right arm and her left arm, stretching out towards Central Railway. I did not want to press, or move anything inappropriately while in that delicate but intimate position. I feared that some excitement might finally show, but with my Reuben Scarf suit and generously billowing trousers, I was somewhat reassured that nothing would betray even this possibility.

In any case, my concentration was focussed on the firm pushing Maugham's 'Of Human Bondage' book held between us. He would not have approved.

I was informed about a dance club on Parramatta Rd near Sydney's Strathfield. Readers might remember the salesman that sold me the Ford V8 also came from that area. He might well turn up at the same place. The place was called Vic's Cabaret, but, like the word 'academy', it was another case of the misuse of words imbued with more than what was actually there. I remember being fascinated by 'Palm Beach' when still back in Holland before the migration episode. The map of Sydney had 'Palm Beach' on it. I used to lay in bed conjuring up waving palm trees, and could not wait to see those. It was a black and white news-reel back in the winter cold of The Hague with natives on tropical islands sipping cool drinks from coconuts underneath beckoning palm trees. After migration, I went to Palm Beach on my scooter. Not a single palm tree in sight! Now, I always thought that cabaret was a bit more than a place to dance in even if it included a small band.

Still, Vic's Cabaret in Strathfield, even without it being a true cabaret in a more European sense, was still a good place to start finding a date. Lots of nice girls would be there, and it just needed a positive attitude and some extra brylcreme. Having straight hair, did not have at that time, the same allure as having a bit of a wave. The TV series '77 Sunset Strip' was responsible for millions of young men imitating the endlessly hair combing, hair-wave owning, wisecracking rock and roll Kookie character. I tried to get this wave, and with enough Brilliantine, hoped that I would also share in the glory of this popular character. Not unlike today with so many young men wanting to be a Bieber clone, or Russell Crowe for the more mature.

The Vic's Cabaret was a short drive from home, and after a good wash and polish of the V8, I was ready and took off. I managed to park within a reasonable distance, and took good note of where I parked. Most streets looked alike, but it helped if one took notice of an unusual feature of where one parked. I took a mental note that the garden next to my car had old white painted rubber tyres around some azaleas. The old tyres were a feature of those times and also kept the weeds out. It was considered a very handy place to put old tyres and often this hint was given in garden magazines. It was one of Dad's pet hatreds, together with the habits of many elderly ladies painting the hair blue or a bright pink. "I saw a lady in the bus today who had pink hair." This is still one of those famous sentences of my Dad still doing the rounds at Christmas time amongst the Oostermans. Dad had great difficulty with adjusting to some odd or strange habits differing from some equally strange habits in his own country. I mean, riding bicycles while wearing a suit, or dipping a raw herring in onions and eating it in full view of pedestrians? All the windows open in full sight of a family eating their dinner? How strange is that?

Striking out on One's Own and First Sex.

I kept up going to Vic's Cabaret, and even expanded my dancing skills by learning the 'stomp', which was of short duration. It was taken over by doing the 'twist'. Looking at old footage of twisting and stomping it all seems to have been so silly. You did not even touch the girl. At least with jiving you threw the girl over your back, or dragged her between your legs, teach her a good lesson. Of course, the hidden message of that dance was for the boy to be dragged between the girl's legs, which happened in some rare instances, but always with the boy facing the floor, never upwards into her billowing skirt. I did not experience that till later. It was with a nice woman from Malta that I finally lost my virginity. "It was on the Isle of Malta where I met you...." No, not really, it was in a boarding house in Sydney's Paddington. The problem with the Maltese woman was not her generosity of spirit or her overabundance of yielding softness, but that she had a husband, a butcher by trade, who kept a loaded shotgun in the wardrobe.

I would be lying to say that dating girls ever led to much more than a furtive kiss given in return for a movie with chocolate Maltesers or a packet of crisps. The Parramatta scooter club that I belonged to folded when motor bikes joined and we could not agree on how to keep the Vespa club at bay. Vespas were outnumbering the Lambrettas, and ran treasure hunts to Palm Beach, to which a few of our own members had been seen going to. There was seething discontent in scooter clubs of the fifties and sixties. Now, of course, this has seeped into the Comancheros and Hells Angels. Today they have guns, and rocks of crystal meth, while we had malted milkshakes.

My own boat's journey on love seemed to flounder forever on the rocky shores of lacking the right personality. The problem was my 'mien'. It was my sombre impression at first sight. Girls had to overcome this. Not an easy task. I could not change what was the essence of my own being. It was at the same time also my best feature. I say this with some confidence because this mien always stood me in good faith later on. The dilemma is that most young girls and boys like good cheer with easy going friendly smiling demeanours. Not many girls seemed to be drawn at my ice-breaking attempts introducing small talk about a demonically violin playing Paganini, or ponderings about the possibility of lives behind the Venetian blinds, or indeed my clear own unique insight in the neglect of Australian cemeteries. I suppose suburbs don't encourage seriousness when the essence of life in suburbs can be so bleak and lacking in a joie de vivre already. The last thing anyone wants on a night out is a dark Schubert like journey of Klage-Lieder with hopeless love buried in the deepest of black watered oceans. This Jeremiah wasn't a Don Juan.

A helping hand was soon knocking at the front-door of my life. A fortuitous move on hindsight was the move away from home to rent a room with board in

Paddington. The landlady was from Malta, and she certainly had a good mien. A bundle of laughs, and generosity expressed by ample heaving and shuddering breasts. On accepting the terms, she immediately cooked me some lovely lamb cutlets with lots of garlic and salted anchovies with rosemary. I remember it so well. "I give you plenty food, Gerard, you are too skinny," she said. The full board was to include bed and all meals with her and family, including the husband, with shotgun as previously touched upon.

Within two weeks of settling in, I was watching TV with her husband sitting opposite from his wife who was seated directly next to me. A few days before she had invited me over to look at some photos of her and husband's wedding in Malta. We were both seated on the conjugal marital bed. I thought it a very friendly gesture, and put it down to Maltese culture and openness. None of that Anglo Saxon reserve. I was happy but a bit nervous. Her bosom was welling up, but with such a large and generous endowment one would have to wear a knight's armour or broad necktie to seek cover. "My husband sick now", she sighed, of which its significance escaped me.

While watching TV and Bonanza with Dad Ben, and the Three Brothers; Adam, Eric (Hoss) and little Joe Cartwright's galloping around the same set of rocks several times, I felt a movement in my left pocket. It was the hand of the Maltese landlady searching me…. Me? It took a while to sink in but was sure her hand wasn't there by accident or looking for my hanky. It was definitely an amorous attempt, sexual even. A tour de force. I was petrified with her husband sitting in the other opposite corner! Did he not know? Where was his gun? However, her hand with gentle but insistent fingers ambushed and overcame my resolve to end it by running away. Au contraire. It was so lovely. I was so excited. I even collegially and conspiratorially leant a bit backwards to give more room to her expert married hand. I had the temerity to lightly stroke her back, keeping a guilty eye out for her husband. What could I do for her? Wasn't this supposed to go twin carburettor for both of us? The horses and Bonanza all but a black and white blur, running berserk for all I cared. A fata morgana that was now really happening to me. The oasis of a real woman.

Can you understand the dread, fear and yet the rewards coming finally to me so longed for and dreamed about? The misery of home life. The rejections of dates and dorky evenings at the cinema with Ben Hur, a Moses with tablets, or some Quo Vadis on a big screen. Here it was, her lovely hand, let the husband shoot me, who cares! Bonanza finished. She got up after her husband had left. "Gerard, get some 'Frenchies' tomorrow, quickly." She smiled and kissed me good night. What a great episode of Bonanza. Next day at 9.01 am I was at the chemist. You will know that condoms at that time could only be given by consent and sold by the chemist himself. He or a she would always be standing, as today, on a podium. I asked for three packets of condoms. All caution to the wind now, and I was on a high. He looked me over and grumpily sold me the condoms. Next morning, I was in bed on the linoleum floor, all shiny and clean. She walked in with husband gone to work (slicing the sausages). She smiled and lifted her dress standing next to my head. Both of us in a single bed, and she was so big. But where there is a will... And that was it. A great initiation by a good woman. I left suddenly after a few days. I did not like the deceit on her husband, and especially not with a loaded shotgun in the wardrobe. The situation was so dangerous. Was he really sick and why this gun? I could not understand that she had the nerve to do this with her husband in the same room. She did like me, and for a year or so she would phone. I knew it was her. She would say, "Gerard, Gerard," but I did not answer her.

Perhaps she too had sadness. Don't we all at times?

Business and National Service in Holland.

With the first sex and my curiosity about it somewhat satisfied, and the Maltese woman with loaded gun in wardrobe fading into Oosterman history, I concentrated with renewed vigour into saving money. I decided to go back to Holland. Readers might remember that I had a little metal box into which I saved as much as I could. Of course, while living at home, I gave all earnings to Mum with her aim of getting our own block of land and own house. This, too, had been achieved within a few years. The garage was now used to rent out to other migrants.

The money came in very handy to top up Mum's income running a very busy household. Who would have thought the take up in the new country had made such rapid progress in such a short time? There was our Mum now collecting rent. The Merchant of Prosperity and now a Rent Lord.

With Frank now coming and going at his whim from the nightmare of what was Callan Park, the atmosphere was often tense again. The first sight of Frank, and we would all just scatter to friends. The impasse between what we thought Frank would and ought to finally get in care, and the rough reality, went on without resolutions. We either had to sign up for his permanent incarceration at a lunatic asylum or put up with Frank basically doing what he liked at the hospital, coming and going whenever, and in whatever condition he might find himself. It was absolutely dreadful, and remained an unimaginable horror, not only to Frank but to the rest of the family. Friends urged my parents to send him back to Holland. Things were supposed to be so much better and more advanced in The Netherlands.

This wasn't easy done with a mentally ill person. He would have to have nursing staff to accompany him, as well as my parents, and how would Frank feel being left in Holland without anyone? A conundrum if ever there was. This would finally resolve itself when both Frank and my parents went back for good to Holland in 1974. They had had enough. On hindsight, that was always the best thing to have done. Pensions and healthcare had improved well above the level of that in Australia. The pension here was 'means and asset' tested. This was achieved in an office of the Social Securities. At one appointment at Social Security, on top of everything else, my parents were asked to empty all pockets and handbags on the table in front of the person dealing with my parents' pension. My Mum never felt so humiliated in her entire life. In Holland, everybody works towards a pension, rich or poor get the basic pension. Not means test. Even today, a pension in Australia is regarded as 'welfare' or 'hand-out', as is unemployment relief, single Mum's income etc., and not as entitlements that civil societies work towards.

It might all have contributed to the fomenting and nurturing of my rich curmudgeon psyche. I really wanted to go back and try to regain what I had left. This was a mistake. But really, making mistakes is a good way of spending years in preparation for adulthood. I always felt that. Never regret a mistake, is my motto. I don't know how, but I had saved up for a trip to Holland within a few years. It was still the old monetary English system of complicated pounds, shillings and pennies. The single boat fare to Genoa, and the train to Amsterdam, was one hundred and ten Australian pounds in 1962/63. The boat trip over was fantastic. Can you imagine; the orchestra playing jaunty music, games of tombola, the daily sweepstake, and lots of young people on their first trip overseas? I do remember the orchestra players being so bored playing the same music, day in day out, week after week, month after month. It was a job so much like everybody had to do a job. Is the chopping of T-bones steaks or the soling of shoes any better (year in year out)?

I also wanted to work in an office, wear a proper suit and carry an attaché case. In Australia, especially during the first few years I was doing piece work on machinery, and clocking up lots of overtime, I wore overalls and steel capped boots, smelling of grease and cheap meat pies. I wondered how it would feel to go to work all spruced up, and nicely attired. I wanted to be seen as a success with something like having importance. I don't know why I thought this would be better suited in Holland. The arrival by train in Holland was without fanfare. There was no one greeting me at Amsterdam's Central Station. I could not have expected it. Even so, I almost thought; can't people see I am a returned migrant from Australia? An absurdity of thought. I moved into a distant uncle's place who had a bed that folded into a wall and who was dying with cancer. He was also an ex-chess master. He was forever berating his ex-wife, and expected me to agree, egg him on with his rancour. I used to mix great lumps of minced-meat with hot spices. He loved it and even felt the spices might cure his cancer. He wasn't used to chilli, but red in the face he would eat lots of the spiced minced steak to the exclusion of everything else. It might well have hastened his final demise.

My old school friends I revisited, and within ten minutes they were watching TV. It had all moved on and they weren't interested in revisiting the past. It had gone by. One of my friends was married, and with two children, gave me sage advice as he unhappily said, 'Never get married.' As is known today, I did, and it was the best thing I ever did! There is so much uncertainty about life. It is all such a risk and bobbing about on tides that can sweep you out to sea in dangerous rips as well as sweep you ashore. We do our best. I haven't yet even come to 'Business and Dutch National service. That will come next time.

Escape from Bank and National Service to Italy's Bolzano.

The trip I took back to Holland was supposed to be permanent. While earning money was good in Australia, the jobs were not enjoyable. My parents had the house built with the help of the Dutch Building society with a mortgage on 'easy terms'. Apart from a mortgage, we also managed to get an electric frypan, and a large timber cased TV on splayed legs, all on easy terms. Life had settled into a routine, and if the criteria of a successful migrant family was ownership of a house and white goods, we had achieved that in a remarkable short period, even if on easy terms. As the rest of the siblings grew older, they too joined the workforce. Each Thursday evening was the keeping of Mum's financial books. Our wages were produced and ledgers were ticked off. The family was prospering and it showed in our diets. Eating meat was now common, and the sauce bottle wasn't quite that much rinsed out anymore. A general relaxing of frugality was now creeping into our lives.

While the standard of living was going up, the standard of my private life remained static and lukewarm. I had saved enough and booked my trip back. As mentioned before, I moved in with my terminal cancer suffering uncle in Amsterdam. He was an ex-chess master, and I had picked up the game in Australia. We shared many a game. He won all of them. He knew the moves and even had names for them. There was a 'Budapest in 1933' move, or the 'Vienna 1867 opening.' He kept on about his previous fame as a chess player while also eating huge portions of my mincemeat and chilli mixture. He kept hoping it was a magic cure for his cancer. It was pitiful. He kept blaming his ex-wife for his misfortune, and when that subject came up, I suggested yet another game of chess. You would have thought he would at least give me a game in exchange for the mince-meat voodoo cure. He never did, and would thrash me mercilessly. I did mix the mince 50/50 with dry bread and an egg to try and bulk it out. He used to wolf it down while rubbing his shoulder in which the cancer was growing, hoping the benefit of the minced meat would shrink the cancer. The heat of the chilli is what he believed would cure him.

I had learned some chess from a good English friend in Australia. He was a very good chess player, but would always give me a handicap of a couple of pieces in order to have at least a fairly equal match. As my game improved the handicap would be reduced. After I arrived in Holland I received a letter he was back in England, and was planning to rent a chalet somewhere in the Italian Dolomites to write words down. He had put an advertisement in the Sud Deutsche Zeitung and received a response from a German Baroness, a 'Frau Johnson' offering him a chalet high in the mountains at Bressanone. He planned to visit me in Holland on his way to take up the offer of the chalet.

Of course, a few weeks before while skiing in Lienz's dolomites, I had already met my future wife. Yet, it still would be a few years before marriage. I had broken my glasses while skiing on a down-hill frosted over molten snow sheet of ice. There was no grip that my skis could hold. I just slid out of control deciding to just drop down on the frozen ice to prevent slamming in a spruce tree. I had a bad nose bleed, and broke my glasses. Fortunately, I had a pair of optical sun glasses to see me through. It was while I was repairing my nose that a young woman asked me if I was all right. I said I was fine and noticed she had taken her skis off and was walking down to the place where I was staying. It was an old farm-house which in winter was let out to skiers called Gribelehof. My Dad's sister had a permanent kind of summer house at the same address.

It is still there, and the same family, the Notdurfter's, are still running it. Amazing after all those years! The young woman had beautiful eyes. I don't know where I got the courage, but I said, "You have beautiful eyes." Her answer floored me, "Yes, I know." She calmly looked back at me as if to see my reaction. My response was surprise. However, there was already a feeling of liking each other. She was encouraging, and even though she said she was aware of her lovely eyes, there was no sense of exploiting the situation. She was really trying something out. We saw each other a few more times before we exchanged addresses and said goodbye.

But back with my uncle and my visiting English friend from Australia, a game of chess was proposed. It was a rather tense game with uncle being opposed this time to a very good player. It turned bad after an hour or so. My friend won. The uncle looked red. He was upset but wanted a return game. The second game he lost, too. My friend bid goodbye to catch the train to Italy. My uncle was really upset. He put the board back again with all the pieces. He remembered exactly the move that he should not have done and played it over, this time making the right move and winning. This gave me some relief. He was not so easy to live with afterwards.

Dutch Bank job, Suit Wearing and Bressanone.

The vexatious uncle now wanted to put all his rancour on my conscience. His loss of two chess games to my friend lumped together with his unfortunate marital experiences seemed to have become part of my doing.

At the time when I was living with him the vexation was still owned and shared by his ex-wife, even though they had been divorced for many, many years. At least I wasn't involved, and remained reasonably free of any blame. However, since my introduction of my English friend and the subsequent chess games, the vexation had now shifted in my direction. I warded the blame off, and felt that at least with my diligence in mixing, and making the mincemeat-bread-eggs and chilli fricandelles it should have been taken into account. I never promised he would be cured from his cancer, and often just agreed that the mixture would do no harm. Especially, since he seemed to enjoy the spicy taste. He was a man in his fifties and ought to have been wiser than me. He suffered from cancer, but that was well before my arrival and the chilli laced patties. It is true, I introduced the chilli as I used it already back in Australia. I had Dutch friends who had been born in Indonesia where the hot chilli is almost an institute. There is some suggestion in medical circles that chilli is somewhat addictive, but that can be only good seeing it contains lots of good vitamins. I mean compared with Coca Cola or sugary drinks. I would rather have a chilli addiction! It was the loss of his chess games that tipped it all over with the vexation sheeted home to me for having introduced him to my friend. Of course, that sort of reasoning is illogical if not unjust, but with people there is not always a straight course in justness or logic. One always has to be on the qui vive for unpredictability, especially in oneself. He might have, deep down, in the recesses of his inner-self, realised that the chilli wasn't helping him but chose to cling to this wrongly held belief in the magic curing quality of it anyway. Perhaps today, I would have had more understanding of his plight. After all, he was in the last few weeks of his life!

As previously explored in some detail, I wanted to have the prestige of working somewhere wearing a suit. It is an odd ambition to have but better to have achieved, and overcome an oddness, than to forever long for it. Nothing gained if not tried. One could question why the wearing of a suit was so important, but I had not really explored working in an office. My jobs since the age of fifteen and a few months were mainly around machinery inside factories, where in the fifties the moods were rather grim and grimy, and that apart from the very fashionable but dubious same sex 'dating' habits between the leering men proving somehow they were hetero-sex after all. With working in the factories, I had a short stint in spectacle making, grinding glass lenses fastened on convex steel chucks by hot pitch with a rotating concave hood on top of the lens; again very dirty work. This time it wasn't dating but the smearing of ultramarine blue dye around the testes of hapless apprentices that was popular. God only knows what went on in England at the time. I am pretty sure this all was an import of initiation ceremonies/rites from the old Mum country as experienced on the convict transport ships.

The very first office job I applied for I got. It was a small branch of The Rotterdam Bank in the East of Amsterdam. It had three people working including me. I was the department book-keeper. The only one. A title that seemed loaded with prestige. I still had my suit from Sydney and had bought a small Hermes portable typewriter on which I furiously learned to type. It took me many seconds just to find an 'a' or an 'f', but on arrival at the bank was shown this enormous bulldozer of an electric typewriter. Even so, I lasted the important first few days, and soon understood that debit and credit were terms that one used. It was the language of any bank. And still spoken about in banks, even today. There weren't any hints of dating or dyeing of testes. The director-manager had his own special chair that could swivel around while cashier and bookkeeper had chairs with fixed seats. The manager smoked cigars, and read a financial newspaper. We had self-rolled cigarettes and no newspaper. My job also included making the tea and leading customers to their downstairs safes where they could count their diamonds or share certificates. The manager had the curious habit of smoking his cigar while tilting back his swivel chair and, exhaling the smoke, wishfully looking up towards the ceiling. It was one of those peculiar habits that most of us have. A kind of personal expression of something. Not unlike rubbing hands together, cupping our chin, or doing a little quick step during fleeting moments of spontaneous and joyful thoughts.

One morning while our manager was exhaling, the chair rotated, and escaped underneath him. He fell back while still holding his cigar in one hand, and the financial paper in the other. The cashier and department book-keeper (me) couldn't stop laughing, but the manager did not appreciate much of the fun. That showed he wasn't ripe for a managerial post. He was unsuitable and given the sack soon after. I kept up catching the tram to work all dressed in my Reuben Scarf suit while holding my all-important attaché case that included documents, and the detailed architectural drawing for a new opera house I had designed for Italy's Milan. Except it held my sandwiches and an apple instead. It also came about that I received a letter that I would be required to enlist for possible National Service, and if found healthy enough do a stint of two years in the Dutch Army. It took me just two hours to pack my suitcase, and bid farewell to my uncle. I did not pick up any due wages or holiday entitlements from the bank. I took the train to Bressanone, Italy, and joined my chess-playing friend, Bernard, in the chalet. The sun shone from then on.

I was cured of my obsession to suit wearing.

Goodbye Suit and Attaché Case.

In life we think we make choices that determine our future. Is that true? One could have turned left or right. So much is due to the unforeseen. The past is never a sign towards the future but only something to mull over in old age and even then, it hardly ever surrenders wisdom or insight. That seems to only come about by a presence of mind while doing the dishes or polishing shoes or writing a few words. I do remember feeling euphoric walking to Central Station in Amsterdam. I must have taken my suitcase and just bought the train ticket to Italy. I walked up the flight of stairs to the platform taking me to the train. It was the absolute right thing to have done. My job at the bank with the daily routine of balancing the books to zero each day had run its course. There is only so much you can do at the end of the day with a nought. It wasn't easy. I had to make sure there wasn't a cent in between. This is the essence of good book-keeping. The cost of a postage stamp could throw my day into turmoil and cost me hours of having to work after hours. No one could go home till the books were zero.

Even the director on the swivel chair had to stay back. All the branches had to give the daily figures to head office which would then print the all-important statements, and post them to the bank's customers. I often used to offer the bank my own money if there was a discrepancy of just a few cents in order to be able to go home. No, that is not what banking is about. The books had to balance. You can see, dear readers, can't you, how my career at a bank had to end? To think that at the very best I too could end up a director and swivel around a special chair. Is that what I had to look forward to? Of course, to become a director could only come about by appointment. The director at my branch wasn't too impressed, especially not when I laughed after he fell backwards with a cigar in his hands. It was doomed. My working and wearing a finely pressed suit at a bank in Amsterdam had come to not much more than before. It wasn't any better than on the Czechoslovakian Capstan lathe in Australia at earlier times. When my friend Bernard had secured a lovely chalet in the North of Italy, I decided to chuck in the job and join him. This decision was made within a split second. The spontaneity of it was breathtaking. I loved it, and still regard this as a turning point in my life. I tend to act rather rashly, which Helvi finds sometimes a bit hard to deal with. Of course, one could question how the bank would feel, not even been notified of my choice to leave. I simply vanished.

They must have enquired at my address of the dying uncle. In any case, the book-keeping must have been done by the director till a replacement was found. I never collected my wages or holiday money as I felt it a just penance for not having given notice. The train trip from Amsterdam to Italy's Bressanone started in rain but ended in glorious sunshine, a good omen. But of that…more to come!

The Period Post Italy but Pre-Finland.

The walk from Bressanone rail-station uphill to Bernard's chalet must have been steep and long. Did I ask for a map or directions? I cannot remember. Consider that in those years suitcases on wheels were yet to be discovered, nor were back-packs as progressive as they are now! Today I see young women with such towering back-packs getting from airports to taxi almost to the point of other bystanders ready to give an ovation. Mind you, even back-packs are now on wheels as well. I must have had a rough idea, and perhaps asked a local for the address. This area was predominantly German-speaking. I was fluent in that language. Bressanone, even though now Italian, used to be part of Austria, and today predominantly Austrian in culture and population. The area is South Tirol.

I do remember reaching the chalet and my friend coming out greeting me. It was so sunny. The view was breath-taking with Bressanone nestling down in the valley, and at the back of the chalet the towering Dolomites climbing forever upwards, glistening with their limestone faces. The chalet was a small, solid white-washed adobe plastered house with ornately carved gables, windows and door architraves, and an extension of the same architecture of the medieval town in East Tirol of Lienz. That's where I had spent time skiing during the winter, and where I had met the girl with the beautiful eyes from Finland. She was the one dabbing my bleeding nose after the ski accident.

It was all such a liberating event. Liberated from the suburban ennui back in Australia with my family and Frank, cursed with schizophrenia. A liberation from wanting to work while wearing a suit hoping for recognition, admiration, or at least something of achievement. A kind of something that young people are supposed to work towards. A career that would cement a solid future, and distinguish one from failure. All those things are not always so clearly defined but yet one grows up with an obligation to fulfil to parents. As those early years passed by I did have a skill to earn some money, and that stood me in good stead. However, the making of money is pretty boring unless compensated or alleviated by an all-encompassing, and absorbing, activity for soul, spirit or psyche.

There are often moments of great significance that are recognised as such at a much later time. The meeting up with Bernard Durrant was one of those life changes that on hindsight proved to be of great influence. In Italy, we met for the second time. I had known Bernard in Australia. It was through him I took to chess playing and reading books and visiting the State library. He gave the advice to run your hand over the back of books at a library, and pick the dustiest books! 'They are often the best,' he said, especially in Australia! Reading books in the early fifties was somewhat neglected in suburban Australia. Everyone was busy getting deposits ready for buying own block of land on which to build own home. Dostoevsky or a Bronte sister wasn't a priority. It was much healthier to play rugby or cricket, spear-tackle opponents. Library visits by young men were rare.

I give you here a very short, and copied biography of Bernard from a website by one of his friends.

"Already serving in the Army, Bernard was recruited by British Intelligence on the eve of the Second World War and was smuggled into Germany, but was soon discovered by the Nazis due to an inadequate cover story. Offered the choice of switching sides or death, he was posted to Alexandria, Egypt, where his brief was to spy on Allied shipping in the Mediterranean. When he arrived in Egypt, he escaped his German paymasters, and eventually made it back to the British Consul in the country. By this time he was considered tainted goods and was shipped back to Britain. Once back on English soil he was promptly imprisoned in the Isle of Man under the Defence Regulation Section 18b, which was used by the Government to lock up more than 1,000 suspected traitors during the course of the war."

Bernard become the lifebuoy that saved me from going the normal way of career, block of own land, and a house in the suburbs. I came so close to it. He got me to accept, and understand, that life ought to be inclusive of beauty and art. He went further, and told me that life is all about exploration and finding what would give the greatest joy and satisfaction. It all gelled and came together, and finally felt that my search for the essential would have to come through expressing what I felt strongest about. It might also relieve me from having to worry about career and job. It was so helpful that there were people like Bernard who had also travelled that same path, and had found that creativity and expressing it was as much a 'normal' part of someone's life as becoming a swivelling cigar smoking bank manager. Apart from all that, we would continue to play chess high up the Tirolean Mountains. I started to paint while Bernard was already writing poetry. Some of which he managed to get published here and there. He had contacts and spoke both German and Italian, which for an Englishman was somewhat unique at that time.

This Business of Earning Money.

While the stay at the chalet high-up at Bressanone was a 'life changing event' (as modern parlance would have it), the question soon arose on how to go forward. While many would agree on 'money doesn't make happiness; happiness doesn't make money either.' Money still needs to be available when buying the corn-flakes, paying the Council rates, and bills. The big question was that while a career, wearing a suit or doctor's coat, wasn't any more on my horizon, how on earth would I survive? Bernard had been working as a tourist guide, and with his knowledge of languages it was a fairly easy and well paid job. He suggested that I do the same. I wasn't sure I was cut out for, or possessed the jovial countenance or enough savoir faire to fulfil the expectations of tourists that had been primed by travel agents to experience Italy in a six hour discounted bus trip through Tuscany and back to Pompeii.

In Australia, I had experienced a long list of many jobs and done a certificate course in quantity surveying. To this day I don't know why I did it, but perhaps it had something to do with my 'suit wearing' ambition period. I would imagine sitting in an office, conversing with Moroccan architects and quantity surveyors, offering expert advice on how to get through the tricky bits of attracting quotes for all the different trades, while rocking on my Finnish Alvar Aalto pressed ply-wood chair. I had already worked on building sites, including working outside buildings from swinging stages. I had also, together with Bernard, worked for painting contractors. Prior to that I was apprenticed for a while in that trade.

In the meantime, I decided to return to my family in Australia. Bernard suggested we set up a business with buff coloured letter-heads and matching envelopes. We both booked a boat from Naples through Thomas Cook travel agents. I remember a Mr Diacomo in Sydney who had arranged my travel to Europe before, but Thomas Cook in Naples was a different animal. Not once did we get an acknowledgement of our requests for a booking to Australia. While Bernard decided to go to Naples to sort out our fares, I decided to stay on in the chalet, and wait for confirmation of the date that we would sail from Naples to Sydney. When the travel confirmation finally arrived I decided to try and catch a lift to Naples. On the first hour of catching a lift, the rubber band through the sole of my thongs snapped. Even despite that, or because of my limping on one thong, I managed to get a lift half way, and caught the train for the remaining distance. Travelling by train in Europe is always fascinating. At most stations in Italy, someone would be walking alongside the train, and for a few hundred lire one could get a hot chicken with crispy bread roll and small bottle of red wine. Absolutely fantastic. Complete strangers would offer bits of their food as well. It was a cultural eye opener, how in Italy, food is shared no matter where or how. One Italian man got up when I arrived in Naples and even adjusted my tie. I could not imagine on the Bowral to Sydney train journey, someone adjusting my tie - even if I was wearing one. The police would probably make an arrest!

The arrival in Naples was as busy and hectic as Bressanone in Tirol was quiet and serene. An amazing rail station and amazing city. Bernard had a hotel room at Piazza Garibaldi right opposite the rail station. It was a very busy part of Naples with coffee sipping, loud talk and lively arguments on the footpaths day and night. The noise level of Naples alone makes it a wonderful and lively city. How a noisy city vibrates and excites! We had just enough money left to see us through the five weeks on-board. We also needed to be able to buy a car on arrival in Sydney for our planned contracting business. Then there was the printing of the buff coloured letterheads with a 'Head-Office' location at my parents place in Revesby.

The trip on board was of course taken up with chess. Bernard met a French woman who took a fancy to him even though her husband was right beside her at all times. She had a very large pony-tail and she played footsy with Bernard while playing bridge. It came to a disastrous head some months later while living in Australia. She decided to cut off this large pony tail and posted it to Bernard as a sign of her profound love and devotion. But as most ship romances flounder on the rocks of on-shore reality, so did this one. She and husband were living in Brisbane, and Bernard in Sydney. We had sat up a good business and were getting reasonable contracts painting blocks of home-units. Sydney was in the middle of a home-unit boom and we caught its head-wind with acute shortages of workers needed to fulfil housing needs. The French girl in Brisbane could not contain her love for Bernard and decided to visit him in Sydney (without her pony tail). My friend took the day off but at the end it was all over. It had run its course. She went back to her husband, and presumably grew a new ponytail.

Who knows?

In Between the Years.

The years between being self-employed, the running of a modest business, and meeting up with Helvi again in Finland in 1965, were not as remarkable as those prior or since that event. I can't remember too many outstanding occasions on par with first meeting her in Austria, arriving and living in Italy after the bank job wearing my suit period, and the boat journey back to Australia. I do remember arriving in Fremantle, again on an empty forlorn Sunday. Nothing much had changed. A deja vu of a return to a bright blue sky, simmering heat and empty streets with the weatherboard houses and their covered up windows staring out like so many blindfolded eyes.

The Sunday Telegraph pages still being blown about. The street dogs scratching. I knew the score.

Another item I remember, was my Dad picking me and Bernard up from the boat at Sydney's Woolloomooloo, and the stalling of his car up a steep hill at a red light. The traffic light turned green and red several times before Dad finally managed to pull away. We were all a bit nervous, and Bernard remarked afterwards that he would not be driven by my Dad again. I was subsequently told by my brother, that once an infuriated driver had followed Dad all the way home, ran out of his car, and told him; 'Right, put them up, you bastard,' and wanted to fight him. That's what his driving had managed to achieve. Dad got a screwdriver and was threatening him as well. It was Mum who stopped the melee and managed to calm things down. Even so, that he passed his driving test to get a driver's license at all at his age was remarkable. Driving his car with his wife gave him great pleasure. I can still see him, washing his car holding the garden hose. In winter, this water in the hose would be frozen, and he used to have to boil a kettle to get the ice from the car window before driving off to his work.

We had the painting business up and running in no time at all. I used to either walk around the job or estimate a quote just by looking at it. If the job was really big, and was designed by architects, I worked out the price by using an extract of a bill of quantities, relevant to the decorating and painting trade. Bernard then drew up and typed a letter of quotation on the before mentioned buff coloured letter head and matching envelope. Once we had done a few jobs we used the success of previous jobs and builders as references as to our expertise and skills to perform the task in time, and within the limits of the quotation. We soon had teams working all over Sydney. Australia certainly proved to be an easy country to set up a business. In Holland that would have been much harder, being riddled with laws, rules and regulations. Australia was and still is an entrepreneur's paradise.

Helvi and I kept in contact sporadically by letter and our hearts grew fonder. I found it hard to believe that such a beautiful and kind girl liked me. I had a photo of her in my wallet and could not get over her smiling face. The photo had her proudly wearing her university student cap. In the intervening years of returning to Australia and going to Helvi in Finland, I managed to again squirrel together a small but important amount of savings. As I was wandering around the inner city one day I noticed a block of town houses going up. I promptly put down a deposit for a small bachelor one room studio on the top floor. It showed a view from that top floor that on reflection I felt could not be really true. I figured it had been taken from the top of the crane that lifted the building materials on the site. I knew about heights, and had worked on swinging stages. I returned to the office of the agents and demanded my deposit back. I then found another much older apartment in an existing building in Kings Cross. It had a bedroom as well as a lift in the building. It had glorious city views from the top floor and was bang opposite the Way-side Chapel. This

Chapel was a hangout for hippies, prostitutes and drug addicts. A haven for the destitute and homeless. A safe place for the lost souls that any society ought to care for, but not always does. In later years, it became a place for the trendies and celebrities to get married. I bought this apartment which included all the furniture, had a gas-run fridge, and small gas stove with oven. I found out that being on the top floor we were right underneath the grinding cog wheels of a very old lift. Never mind - it was perfect. If I remember right, it cost seven thousand seven hundred Australian pounds.

Less than two years later, Helvi and I would be living in it!

The Run-Up to Marriage.

The words have been lean lately. The school holidays are the bane of and blame for the lack of words. I am too much of an egotist to try to put down words under difficult circumstances. Multitasking falls to those who are unselfish and can spread goodness and sweetness around no matter what. They even do it better. I forego flowing words in order to make pancakes or fry speck for the grandkids. It could just be an excuse to take a break. Regroup! I am not a multi-tasker. Ask my wife! Do words not deserve a holiday? I mean, you can tell words are suffering when you hear people say 'awesome' and even 'absolutely'. Just now I heard on the news, something needing 'a paradigm shift in attitude'. The popularity of 'stuff like that' is on the wane. Thanks to our PM, T.

Abbott, though, there has been a resurgence of 'absolutely' and making things 'crystal clear'! Saying 'obviously' twice in each new sentence is now being patented by Tony Abbott, our Rhodes scholarly Prime Minister of funny sayings, absolutely!

The school holidays usually involves both good and bad. The good is self-evident. To have domestic life with the sound of children. Pillows on the floor. Tripping over shoes that somehow find themselves in front of your step no matter what direction you take. Despite the shoes, it was fine to have them around again for a few days. They are a font of delightful expressions which any writer would use and exploit. They are both still verbally agile and imaginative like most children are. I pray they keep this and not allow it to be knocked out by maturing into stiff and compliant adults. You know the kind who feel that the ability to say 'please' and 'thank you' is enough to get you through. Maybe! But a good 'fuck you' and 'piss off' to bullying adults might stand them in just as good a stead. What is in a word? A lot!

So back to my marriage. As the painting contracting got more and more colourful, with teams working all over Sydney, the post-Italy period was put to good use. I had bought an apartment in Kings Cross. I did not actually live in it. I let it out, and used the rent to pay the mortgage. It proved to be another prudent move in my life. I also continued on with painting pictures. I had taken a painting course locally in Parramatta. This was the suburb some years before, where I used to meet fortnightly as the secretary of the 'Parramatta Scooter Club.' Readers that held on to my blog so far, would know this club disintegrated when Vespa and Lambretta did not see eye to eye. There was even someone with a Norton 500 cc single cylinder motor bike allowed to join up.

The painting course was run by Ronald Peters, a man who abhorred what was going on at the NSW art gallery. Modern paintings were being hung and crowds would peer at them incomprehensibly. They did not make any sense to him either. He warned us to avoid modern paintings like the plague. He taught me to start with sky; 'A dark blue at the top of the canvas and lighten the colour as you go down,' he said. 'It will create distance.' Gum trees always featured. 'Put some dappled highlights on the bark'. We were urged to follow his own painting at the front of the class. Step by step! It was the period when D H Lawrence's Lady Chatterley's lover was still banned. Portnoy's Complaint was whispered about on corners by men wearing rain-coats. Today, publishers are wringing their hands. Readers are secretly and under the blankets reading words for free on Kindle, freeloading, copying and swapping! Book shops now are closing down. Real book readers are becoming rarer and Borders have shut shop. Celebrity and sport books are still being sold, and some bookshops are offering three books for the price of two. I see the smiling open mouthed Jamie Oliver still staring out at Super Markets, but for how much longer? After all those years, do people still need to know how to cook a T-bone? Milan Kundera, who has heard of him? A cricketer was killed by a ball some weeks back and his wife was offered a state funeral! No such offer for the funeral of Australian Nobel prize winner author, Patrick White, some years ago.

I gave the landscape class a miss even though I was surprised how nice my pictures looked. The dappled effect on eucalypt bark very much liked. Some of those little paintings I took with me in a suitcase on my way to Helvi's Finland. For a few months I did an art course with John Olson and Robert Klippel. Both were at the revolutionary edge of breaking away from the traditional art scene in Australia. Their work created heated scenes at art galleries with people trying to take them to court. Clashes of traditional art lovers with the young and anti-Vietnam war protesters. A portrait by Dobell was taken to court on the grounds it was a caricature. The artist won. Our letter writing to and from Finland increased, and not just in numbers. Exchanges of photos and sweet whisperings became intensely loving. The tyranny of distance could only be overcome by a boat journey. Helvi still needed to do a few more exams but I proposed anyway, and...she accepted. How glorious! I remember it well. Exultation followed by booking a boat to Italy's Genoa in 1965

.On The Boat to Turku-Finland.

There is a Writer's Festival on this week in Bowral. They seem to pop up everywhere now. I have never been to one yet. They are at the drop of a hat (or book) in Bali too. Each day this week something to do with books and writing is on somewhere in this region. Helvi has read the pamphlet. It combines writers and their published books with lunches and sumptuous dinners. The prices range from twenty five to one hundred fifty dollars per person. A large banner is hung across the main street in Bowral advertising the event. You wonder if writer's festivals are in cahoots with restaurants to bolster trade.

There are two book shops in Bowral. One right next to the other. They have been here for years. Both often feature the same books. Mainly cooking. Lots of colour photos of pork crackling, almost to the point that the books seem to sizzle in sympathy. This week both shops feature at the Writers Festival. A good selection of known and unknown (by me) writers will grace the festival to talk to and answer questions by interested readers and budding writers. The Writer's Festival advertisements also feature in the windows of chemist shops vying for space with the incontinence pads for the mature. Is there a link between reading books and incontinence? Does a Paracetamol tablet help? Does reading give cause for intestinal hurry syndrome? I must investigate. I am not sure that if having a book published, and the deal includes also sitting at a dinner table and fielding questions from eager readers, would be worth it. How keen would I be to go through that? Would I not remain mute, staring at my plate with the rare-cooked beef-mignon and Kipfler spuds? Or would I do a chameleon and change in a stand-up raconteur? There are those who write brilliantly and also perform well in public. I don't.

Some years back I was asked if I would like to be interviewed on radio by someone called 'Red'. The radio program was a light early breakfast kind of show. It was meant to be filled with laughter and happiness. (I should have been suspicious.) The interview was a result of something I had written on the National Broadcaster, the ABC. I had never heard of him but my daughters had. I remember sweating all night on what I would say and how my answers would come across. I knew the date and time when this short few seconds interview would take place, and had settled in a comfortable chair an hour before the interview. I had also taken a shower, brushed my teeth. I was phoned up by 'Red's' secretary and advised to turn my radio off. A time lapse would only confuse me! I never heard or listened to the interview. It was over in a flash. Thirty seconds of fame just fleeted by. Many years before, I was interviewed on TV about my experiences having undergone a vasectomy. Millions watched this, including my Mum. 'How is your performance now, post vasectomy, Mr Oosterman? Has it improved, or are you still recovering?' I was asked by the smirking but attractive Channel 9 girl. Did I shrink? The local butcher had watched it, too. 'You had it cut off?' he asked, while packing the snags. Confidence is a strange animal. Fortunately, no interviews since.

Before boarding the boat to Finland I packed my suitcase with some of my small paintings of gum trees and blue skies. Was it the same suit that I wore in the Bank during my stint in Amsterdam? I have forgotten. I do remember lots of Australians on their way to England for their first experiences of a different country. A few passengers are worth mentioning. One was a large stomached Australian man with huge feet clamping equally large rubber thongs between enormous toes. Each day one would find him on the deck giving court to many listeners, all of whom seemed to crack tinnies of beer all day long. As the day grew in tandem with the mountain of tax-free empty tinnies, it became more and more raucous. On one particular day he held forth on the item of 'love'. 'Oh love,' he said dismissively. 'It is nothing but something with hair on it!' This resulted in a huge outburst of mirth by his disciples (mainly men), almost an applause, certainly an approval. And then... he did not come on deck anymore. Questions were asked. He had died midway between Aden and Port Said. I wondered if he died wearing his thongs?

Another person on-board was a Finnish boy named Pirkko. He was on his way back to Finland for good. He did not like it in Australia. He had worked at Mount Isa, a large mining town, and was somewhat reticent and shy, the opposite of the garrulous Aussies. I confided in him that I was going to Finland to marry a Finnish girl and showed him a photo of Helvi. He was impressed and spoke about his family and background. The Finns are known for avoiding small talk and Pirkko was no exception. We would spend hours talking in silence. He disappeared soon after we both arrived by ferry on the

Finnish shore from Sweden's Stockholm. I thought that he very much wanted to meet a girl from his home country. From Genoa I took a train to Stockholm and then the ferry to Finland. As the boat berthed at Finland's Turku, I looked down from the deck of this huge ferry, and she was there, waiting for me. She looked up and recognised me too.

She smiled.

Finland-Suomi.

Travelling in the mid-sixties did not yet involve threatening gun carrying Border Protection Guards nor queueing at all sorts of gates to get on board a boat, plane or train. I never had to take shoes or belt off, hop through metal detectors or be padded down for concealed weapons under my armpits or between my legs. Or, if they existed, I can't remember. I suppose a passport was sometimes glanced at, perhaps even stamped, after which the train guard would dip his cap, say thank you, and move on to the next carriage. Of course, we did lug suitcases, for which those handy swivelling wheels and extended handles still had to be invented. The suitcases of that period had two chrome plated snappy locks for which a key was used that was so universal it opened almost every suitcase. Even so, we felt safe travelling. Travellers smiled and were tolerant.

Finally arriving in Finland, and getting off the large overnight ferry, must have been smooth. Perhaps I did have to show my passport. All I had eyes for, somewhat nervously, was for the girl with the smile. The Mona Lisa who promised to me as I did her. She wore a lovely two piece sienna coloured outfit. I definitely did not wear my suit! It was mid-summer but not just the season. All of Finland seemed braced in cheerful golden hues. We embraced, took each other in, held hands as we walked slowly to the railway station. I must have walked lopsided holding her hand in one and a suitcase in the other. We stopped somewhere, had a coffee. A lot was going on. It had been a while since our first encounter skiing and a bloody nose resulting from the icy fall. That exchange; 'You have beautiful eyes,' and her unnerving answer, 'Yes, I know.'

We kept in contact by writing, frenetically towards the end, before my departure from Australia to Finland for our marriage. At the arrival in Finland we met each other for real and possibly forever. Looking at each other's facial expressions, glancing shyly to study the other's nose in profile, the chin, feeling each other's hands... and in particular, I finally got to look into those beautiful eyes and enjoy especially, her lovely smile. The way we walked and talked naturally, both comfortable in our skins as well as with each other made me confident that we were making the right decision in getting married. It was beautifully serious and often fortunately hilarious as well, wholesome... as a river flows quietly into the ocean. Still is.

My knowledge of Finland was scant. It was the forgotten corner of Europe, and unlike Sweden and Norway wasn't much on the world's horizon. I knew by looking at the map trying to find the village where Helvi grew up that it was a huge country, sparsely populated. It had a land climate with surprisingly warm dry summers and long cold winters. I knew that its architecture was modern, and that it had a very strange language with long words that I could not link to anything. The long words became comprehensible, only after some time when I learned that, unlike English or Dutch who use many words to form a sentence, the Finnish language links many words into one long word for meaningful sentences. Suffixes, adjectives, pro-nouns, you name it; they are all joined into the one word without even using articles or prepositions. Perhaps this unique language developed out of the long winters. The need to be sparse and economical, no waste of energy, preserve the good. I would like to think that it is so. Academics claim differently. There is a link to Hungarian and Turkish languages. The mind boggles. It is surprising the language survived at all. Ownership of Finland wavered often between Sweden and Russia throughout its history.

It was soon discovered that my Dutch passport wasn't enough identification for a marriage. Even though I was a resident of Australia, I needed much more paper work done. A date of the wedding had been set to coincide with all the Finnish family members which was extensive. Helvi came from a family of nine children, of which she was almost in the middle. My parents in Australia were hoping for a wedding in Sydney! The date was shifted several times. It became so hard that when all the paperwork was finally done, including a finger-print extract from Australian police proving I was not a known (or unknown) criminal, that we just decided to marry in a registry instead. The wedding dress was dyed in red and given to one of Helvi's sisters! Afterwards, we had a photo taken. I haven't been able to find this photo. There are so many boxes of photos with so many albums to go through and so little time. Do people actually go over old photos?

We rented a cottage on a frozen lake with outside sauna. It was in
Ankeriasjarvi.

During the previous process to get married in full regalia, including a big party afterwards, with guests and laden food tables, wild dancing including the tango or polka, I remember going to the local parish and asking the Lutheran priest to marry us. He was a good man but very careful, he did not speak English. He kept rubbing his chin and saying, 'Niin, niin,' which meant translated, 'Well, well, or so, so.' 'I have to think this over, come back in two weeks' time, I'll give it more thought.' After two weeks we returned to this good man. But, again the priest rubbed his chin and again said, pensively 'Niin, niin!' This time he had a thick book in front of him. Perhaps he wanted to put more weight to his eventual answer in marrying us, and showing us seriously investigating the problem of marrying a foreigner. The Lutheran church in Finland is strong, a very important part of Finland and its culture. He meant well. He did not want to make a mistake. Perhaps he was worried that he might marry a rogue of a non-believer. A scoundrel from Australia. He was not totally unjustified in thinking that. The third time back it was still, 'Niin, niin,' while rubbing his chin in between huge silences.

We got married, eventually, but at a registry! And by that time the summer had passed. It was now mid-winter, and what a winter. A few day-times the temperature dropped to -34c.

'Nakemiin,' My Beautiful Suomi But Back To Reality!

There is no wedding video. The bride did not swoon or got swept away by a Sharif-like groom on horseback with manes flying, galloping along the shoreline of the Gulf of Bothnia. Instead, both of us spent some weeks in a cottage at Ankeriasjarvi. We made lots of pancakes, and lived off smoked eel and the fruits of love. I tried to catch fish in order to prove I would be a good provider for the future. After hacking a hole in the frozen lake and lowering my fishing line, all I got was frozen feet and hands. I improved a little, a day or so after, when I promised to make her tea in a billy in 'the Finnish bush'. I explained this was a cultural initiation ceremony in Australia for all newlyweds. Omitting to tell her that often it was a string of beer cans being pulled along a VW Kombi van instead. I made the best of the present romance enjoyed on the shores of a Finnish lake, sipping Billy tea.

When the day warmed up to a balmy -20c and a shy sun peeked a bit yellow, we both walked towards the edge of the frozen glistening lake with the pine forests protecting it. In no time did we find enough kindling to make a fire. Snow in the billy can for pure water, and soon above the smoking fire. We had a cup of tea. 'Bob is your uncle,' I mentioned unthinkingly. Even though this latest was said in German, Helvi did not get it, but gave a smile anyway. 'Bob ist ihr Onkel? Aber ich habe kein Onkel Bob,' she said. It was then that we realised that a better common language would have to come about in bits and pieces.

There were so many funny episodes, we laughed our heads off in between.

One day, we went to a piano concert performed in the nearest city named Jyvaskyla. There was a train service between Ankeriasjarvi and Jyvaskyla. Helvi must have got a timetable. We had walked between the cottage and train station a few times during the day, so we thought we could venture the same after the concert finished, which would have been close to 11pm. I forgot what piano concerto was being played or the name of the pianist. It might have included Sibelius music as an extra. It should have! At the time I only learned about J P Sibelius through Helvi. My knowledge about Finland was so limited. All I wanted to know better was the girl from Finland at the expense of everything else. The hall in which the concert was held was designed by Alvar Aalto. He was one of the world's best known architects and no wonder, his buildings are beautiful, and so is almost everything designed in Finland. Simple, utilitarian and a pleasure to look at, always beautiful, never kitsch.

Helvi at Ankeriasjarvi train-stop.

We notified the guard on the train we wanted to get off at Ankeriasjarvi. It all seemed rather simple. That's how train travel was at the time I was there. The train would have stopped at around 11.30 or close to midnight. It was pitch dark, and quite a step down onto the timber platform. Perhaps someone helped us to lower ourselves. We had taken a torch to lead us back through the snow and along the path that ran along the lake's edge. I could add that there was a gentle moon reflecting itself on the white frozen lake and also helping us along back to our cottage. It was a walk that could never have been repeated. It would have been a cliché. Our little cottage was still warm and we put on another log. Perhaps we had tea or coffee before hitting the sack. A great unforgettable evening. We both liked the adventure and excitement of that walk during that arctic winter's evening along the lake having listened to a wonderful concert.

Alaharman Pojat ja Tytot; A Burning Ship.

The six months or more that I lived in Finland could easily fill a book. I haven't even reached the Kalevala. Finland's national epic of which so much Finish culture, music and design is derived from. Let me make amends and give you at least the basics of what the Kalevala is about, and I copy from Wiki:

"is a 19th-century work of epic poetry compiled by Elias Lönnrot from Karelian and Finnish oral folklore and mythology. It is regarded as the national epic of Karelia and Finland and is one of the most significant works of Finnish literature. *The Kalevala* played an instrumental role in the development of the Finnish national identity, the intensification of Finland's language strife and the growing sense of nationality that ultimately led to Finland's independence from Russia in 1917."

And yet, despite all that beauty and creativity, Finland remains a country with a rather reticent self-image. It doesn't easily boast or do unnecessary head-stands or engage in world-stage pole vaulting. The Ankeriasjarvi hut with outside sauna and water-well with its lovely lake had to come to an end. Love alone might never end, but finally also needs more than walking along water's edge or hacking holes in ice in the hope of catching sad eyed and lonely fish. Has anyone ever experienced the delights of throwing water on boiling hot stones inside a wooden hut lined with fragrant pine? Taking a Sauna in Finland is as close as getting to a religious experience as possible.

We had bought some paints. I did a few paintings while waiting for news from the local Australian embassy to gain a residency permit for Helvi to live in Australia. We were given an appointments for interview but when I showed the immigration man at the Embassy our buff coloured letter head with my parents address for 'Head-Office' within seconds the consul assured us there was no problem. Australia was desperate for building and painting contractors. He almost gave us free shovel and wheel- barrow to take with us on board the ship.

We then booked the boat. It was again one of the Italian-Line Flotta Lauro boats, either the 'Roma' or its sister ship 'Sydney'. The original idea was to live in Finland where I would paint pictures and Helvi teach. We had looked at a few timber houses in the countryside, but after a while decided to delay this plan, go to Australia for a few years instead, and build up some capital. While first waiting for all paperwork to be finalised for a grand wedding and then just ditching it for a registry marriage, we now waited for all approvals allowing us entry to Australia. Helvi was never too fussed about conventions. I guess another reason we clicked together so well. Even so, the move to leave home and hearth was hard and very brave. She had already moved away from her family home for some years when she had to live close to her gymnasium and after to the university. She shared a house with her brother who was also studying. At weekends she travelled home to the farm to be with her very large and extensive family.

The village she lived in was peopled mainly by her Dad's brothers and other close relatives, with the farm houses clustered cosily together and the farm land nestled around this village. Some crops were grown, some had milking cows and most also produced timber. I remember visiting her Dad's sister just a short walk from the farm. She was married to a man who had lived for many years in Canada and spoke English with a strong Canadian accent. His name was Antti. He told me an interesting and amazing story of why he went to Canada in the first place. His wife was always a bit anxious when he spoke to me in English. Her name was aunty Maija. The main event when visiting family and friends was to have coffee. Coffee drinking in Finland is a national past-time, together with eating 'pulla', a kind of cardamon semi-sweet cake revered as the essence of much Finnish baking. If you are offered coffee and pulla you are in good hands. Sometimes cream is put on top and coffee is sweetened with cubes of sugar. (Readers might remember many years later on the hot train between Moscow and St Petersburg a kind and buxom woman offered me those same cubes but dipped in Absinthe after she found out I painted pictures. The same woman also dabbed her generous bosom with Eau de Cologne with an embroidered hanky. Oh, how those memories linger! Was the number of that Cologne 711 or 911? It is so confusing now.)

It was within a few weeks before our departure when a telegram arrived telling us a fire had broken out on our ship cancelling our trip. But, as compensation, were offered a first class voyage to Australia on their other Flotta Lauro ship a couple of weeks or so later. When the time came, we said goodbye. We walked out of Helvi's farm. We somewhat sadly now carried suitcases to take ferries and train to Genoa to catch the boat to Sydney. Half of this boat held about 20-30 passengers in its first class, the rest of the boat, hundreds of migrants, mainly Italian and later on Greek migrants. One of the many perceived advantages, apart from having so much space, was dining, almost every night with the captain and his top crew. Luckily we had a nice crew and the captain was popular on both parts of the boat. We would at times go to the other half and have more fun with so many more people around. We shared a small round dining table with a sophisticated elderly Italian couple on their way to visit their pianist son in Melbourne. We also drank a bottle of white Italian wine every night called 'Suave' with our dinner. One can still buy this wine today. The Italian couple were very nice. One high point, at least in the case of Helvi, was that the very charming, debonair and white uniformed captain used to ask Helvi for a dance. I could tell Helvi loved it. They were a nice couple and looked stunning. Helvi is a natural when it comes to swaying and dancing. While on the other hand I danced as if still following the painted Phyllis Bates Fox trot steps on the parquetry floor in Sydney. I danced with the generously endowed Italian wife of the husband that we shared the dining-table with.

It was a great sea voyage.

Kanimbla-Hall, Pott's Point, Sydney.

Little needs adding to the previous story of how we finally ended up on a boat to Australia, sailing first class, dining with an Italian couple, and Helvi dancing with the captain. Perhaps I should add as a minor detail that I also won the ship's chess competition, with the final match being played with the ship's doctor. He was supposed to be a very good player. Boasting a bit here, but one might be forgiven. One should never resist the temptation to live off minor triumphs in life as much as possible. You just never know what tragedy might be waiting around the corner! One other memory just bubbling up right now was the teaching of English to some of the Greek migrants on the boat. An Australian immigration officer on-board asked for volunteers to teach English. Helvi suggested I should offer to do just that. I was given a class of Greek people, mostly men, but also a few young couples. All were eager and keen. I have never met a more joyfully optimistic mob of Greek people. The teaching was simple. I knew no Greek and they knew no English. It was done by pointing and writing. There is a name for this type of teaching, but I can't bother looking it up. Time is of the essence, and what is in a name?

I started narcissistically pointing to myself and at the same time saying 'Gerard,' which was followed by everyone saying their names as well. This then became, 'My name is…' followed by the whole class repeating it. The fun really started when progressing to trades and jobs. Hammering down, became a carpenter. Slapping around with a brush, a painter, and so on. It turned out many of the men were all of the trades. They were all cobblers, butchers, you name the trade, and the same hands would fly up. This was cause for great hilarity. Talk about a keen lot of people. No wonder so many became successful in Australia. One could ask why did they chose to leave a country that millions flock to each year, especially with a population so given to spontaneous dance, laughter and happiness? I noticed the same with the Italians. Of course, grinding poverty and unemployment endemic in many Southern European countries could be the answer. Even so, there did not seem to be that same expression of cheer and good humour in countries where far better material conditions did exist. Has anyone ever caught public transport in the UK? Those grim faces holding onto their umbrellas as if a stolen stash of gold!

I reflected how within a few weeks those happy Greeks would be drawn to working, saving, and enjoying their new life. Now there would be unlimited plates laden with fetta, lamb and spinach. No shortage for the kids and....own house, even own business, a milk bar called Stavros with photos being sent back to the relatives in Greece. Did the boisterous laughter continue in Australia as then still on the ship? Leave the pensive reflections well alone, 'My name is gerard.' What are you hoping for?

Sydney Harbour. 1966

We arrived in Fremantle. Of course, on yet another Sunday. We sauntered through the hot lonely barren streets. It was my third Sunday in Fremantle. Not much had changed. The continuation to Melbourne was through The Great Australian Bite. The enormous swell parallel with the boat made even the crew churn up their meals, let alone the passengers. Many paper bags strung up along the corridors and stairs. Sea sickness is a cruel part of any sea voyage. Even though most passenger boats have stabilisers fitted, they were of little use. Most remained in their cabins, heaving, retching miserably away in private. Of course, Helvi and I were exempted from all this misery. Proudly arm in arm we would pace the decks. Our red faces into the fierce wind.

Nonchalantly defiant to Zeus and Poseidon. No sea too rough, no woman (or man) so tough! The dining rooms all but for a hardy few, deserted. Tables fastened, and piano roped down in the corner. Those few passengers that did turn up ate off plates that had been put on wet plastic sheets to give traction to prevent them from sliding about. We ordered bacon and eggs to a pale looking waiter. Our Italian table companions absent, as was the captain.

After Melbourne, a more normal city with people about, and then …Sydney. That beautiful glide through the heads, and then to the Opera House in full progress, cranes sticking up as if waving to the newcomers. Finally arriving at my parents' place. They immediately liked Helvi. My Mum thought we would live in the garage for a while. She had put up cheerful new curtains, a red and white checked cotton strung along the top of the louvered windows, facing the street. We slept there just one night. Next day, we went to the city, including my little apartment in Kings Cross or Pott's Point. It had become vacant just before our departure from Finland. Helvi immediately liked it. We decided to live there instead. It was fully furnished, even had all the pots and pans, cutlery and fridge. Even its name, 'Kanimbla Hall,' seemed attractive. It was really a bit of a no choice. I mean, the no-ones' land of the suburb, neither country-side nor city. The choice was for city with life.

We moved in next day. It was so exciting.

Life at the Cross.

Our move to Sydney's Kings Cross was decided the next day. It needed no considering really. We walked around the main shopping street, looked at the apartment of Kanimbla Hall, which as mentioned before, Helvi really liked. She has always been able to see the potential in any of our homes. Perhaps that sense of good proportions and making the best of any given space, as well as this undefined art of recognizing what makes things look good or awfully ugly. It seems to be the domain of a Finn. Perhaps it is also a genetic thing. I don't think you can teach good design if the eye for the visual is absent nor make a good writer by teaching cobbling words together when they enter a brain better equipped for understanding Rock-a-Billy or betting on galloping horses. The idea that we are all capable of doing amazing things if only given the encouragement together with being diligent enough, and have the determination to succeed, might be over-rated. We do the best we can and the philosophy, 'and may the devil take the hindmost,' always a good thing to keep in mind. Just in case! (*Or Love Lies a-Bleeding*, 1611 :) Does it really matter? It is in the doing, and we can all do, surely?

In the mid-sixties, Sydney did have a few areas where multi- culture and a cosmopolitan life existed. Now, of course, almost everything has 'a life style', even buying a house or an electric knife sharpener, is imbued by its promise to 'add' to your lifestyle. The advertising world has managed to make us all fear in missing out on the promised land of the magic lifestyle and have hordes of people rushing to Harvey Norman and those Meccas of consumerism, the shopping Malls. It is all proof on how we are goaded into leading our lives never quite fulfilled. We all so keenly want to get at this so desired 'lifestyle.' We sink somewhat deflated into our latest acquisition, the reclining sofa, while watching Neighbours on a three metre barking mad wide flat screen TV. It resists all our efforts, no matter how we shop till we drop, and of course drop, we finally do. The ultimate 'life-style' finally achieved with ashes to ashes!

Kings Cross was at the very heart of what life is capable of throwing up. There were artists, vagabonds, drug addicts, criminals, and smiling red rouged but kind prostitutes. Mums with babies in prams and some normal Dads. It was a friendly and safe place then. Perhaps still is! It had book shops, and a great butcher shop named 'Hans Fleischmeister' that sold continentals, including rookworst, sauerkraut, and marinated olives, as well as prosciutto, preserved red cabbage, and cooking apple in Hak glass containers with many other strange and twisted looking delicatessen. On a Saturday morning the queue would spill over onto the pavement and the smell of this shop lured many to venture out of the apartment blocks, like the town-crier of earlier times. There were also nightclubs and strip joints, spruikers and American soldiers on RI leave from Vietnam or from strange wars fought somewhere else. Many looked for romance but compromised with a hurried love for sale. We knew by sight some of the girls who scored a trick, and nodded to us with a smile. We were part of a world that still walked the pavements. A blushing fountain depicting a dandelion flower seed head was the very centre of our chosen domain. It was such a vibrant area to live in. A little park had seats on which the book reading pensioners of the time could be seen reading or nodding. Sometimes both. The library and Franklyn supermarket were edged on this lovely green refuge. Kings Cross was to be our home for a few years. Both of our daughters were born at the local St. Luke's hospital at Kings Cross.

Helvi transformed the apartment by lifting the 'wall-to-wall' under which we found a perfect hardwood floor which we partially covered with a rug. One of my paintings was hung on the wall together with a Finnish wall-hanging, a wedding present, now hanging in our present home. We also replaced the apartment's crockery with the Finnish Arabia brand. We bought a very nice set of cutlery in a wooden box made in Austria. The Bakelite radio and laminated kitchen table and bed-head replaced with nicer looking accoutrements. Also bought was a black and white small TV on which we used to watch a quiz contest 'Pick-a Box' with Bob Dyer, and his excruciatingly irritating wife with the name 'Dolly,' who would come on-stage to drool, 'Oh yes, Bob,' in a strong accent, over and over again whenever she was beckoned by Bob. There was a world champion contest between the world's best factually informed with also the most and best of the retentive memories at call on this 'Pick a Box'. It was between an Australian named Barry Jones and a Finn. Barry Jones won and became a politician later on in life, which shows you how pure knowledge can be a bad thing.

These were our Kanimbla Hall years. Very good years they were too!

Children, Tripping Over and Business.

After we settled in Kings Cross there was a flurry of marriages in the Oosterman clan. My friend, Bernard, married a Japanese girl, and went to live in Japan. I continued with the painting business on my own. One of my brothers married a girl from Russia but born in Peru, another from Polish background, my sister married a man born in Germany with just one who married an Australian. I, of course, married a lovely Finn. Apart from my brother who married an Aussie and whose wife has died since, we all are still married to our first love. Times were hectic, all racing to get home and hearth together as well as bonnie babies. There were nappies and the smell of them. Toys on the floor. A variety of bassinettes and other bouncing contraptions that we would all easily trip over. They were the years when tripping over was normal and totally safe. Of course, now a fall could easily result in an ambulance racing over to lift you on a stretcher, and to a hospital. A kind nurse putting on the gloves and a worried doctor looking you over. I haven't as yet reached that stage yet, but it will come about! Helvi urges me to take a firm hold of the handrail coming down from the computer upstairs. It pays to be careful! I sometimes wish that recklessness could continue. It was such a part of being young. Reckless and foolish. Now we play it safe, and pretend to be wise, but really just give in to ageing, play it secure, getting old, sip our coffee, and remind each other to take medicine. We have learned our lessons.

It seems odd that when we were so young and reckless we took our chances. Yet, so much was at stake. One mistake could easily have resulted in having to pay for it over the rest of our natural life. Yet, now that we are old and with our lives more behind than in front. We have far more good and solid reasons to be reckless. Throw caution to the wind. What is there to lose? What is holding us back? Do a bungy jump or fight a crocodile, live in Bali or Amsterdam. We might just, with luck, squeeze in a couple of years more or so. Of course, many of the old do amazing things still, but, by and large, we have become more cautious, and play it safe. I never ever thought I would reach that stage. Yet it is has come about. Even so, we still have no insurance of any kind except third party property car insurance which I suppose is proof of some lingering recklessness. Harking back to youthful risk taking. I mean, does one not get buried without having funeral insurance? Does it matter? Mozart got buried in a pauper's grave. Perhaps, that is just bundied about to encourage budding composers to keep on trying, regardless of fame or fortune.

But going back (to those years of recklessness), and having settled down. Oosterman families were sprouting up all over the place. Our first was born within a couple of years after arrival in Sydney. Our second daughter two years after that, delivered by the same doctor named Holt. I renewed previous contacts and gained quickly new jobs. Some years later, I won some really substantial contracts, including the painting of the extensions to the NSW Art Gallery and the International Flight kitchen at Sydney's airport. I tried as well to keep on with painting pictures and even had, optimistically, bought a huge fifty metres by two metres roll of raw cotton canvas together with varied sizes of stretchers on which to span, and make canvasses ready to paint. I was an optimist. Both of us supporting each other. What could go wrong? They were very good years.

Many good years were yet to come.

The Years of Gertrude's Cottage.

The meandering through life's travels and travails will continue for as long the memory will keep on serving the details, or at least the general gist of them. After a while, dates become irrelevant. It is the memory of events that count. This writer is not going for a PhD nor fame. A couple of 'likes' will suffice and makes him smile. I just read that cooking chefs are now more esteemed and held in a higher limelight than writers. And yet, most chefs on TV shows don't really say much more than 'mm' or 'nice, really nice,' at the most. Of course, they fill the program with beautiful scenery. Why cooking has to be done with the Austrian Dolomites in the background or in the middle of the Mekong River is baffling. Perhaps it spurs us on to travel rather than grab the mortar and pestle. It is perplexing though how cooking and watching cooking has now overtaken reading Vladimir Nabokov or Chekov. Perhaps all this is due to an ageing population wearing multifocal glasses! Many people also go to bed with food platters, (including smoked eels) instead of a book.

After our second daughter was born, the apartment became too small. We happened to look at The Sydney Morning Herald with an advertisement for a cottage for sale. The cottage for sale was 'Gertrude's Cottage'. It faced the harbour and had a goat. The advertised price was $12.500. We knew this was ours right from the start. I don't believe in premonition or future or fortune telling devises. I took a drive to the address which was right on the harbour of Sydney in Balmain, which was an area that used to be 'working class and 'cut-throat' territory, belonging to thieves, drunkards and Irish Catholics. I say 'used' to be, because it had become a bit of a low cost housing area for students and artists. It was changing, and in an upward transit.

Gertrude's Cottage

Even so, the rabbito men were still selling them from the back of the truck, rifles on the front seat, albeit in its final years. The milkmen and bread delivery were also a daily event. I am running ahead somewhat now. The Gertrude Cottage was as charming as I had imagined it to be with a large living-dining-kitchen area, with the bath all out exposed in the lounge area. I knew Helvi would love it and she did. Upstairs were two small bedrooms. The whole cottage was weatherboard, very old, and one corner had sunk on its foundations which made the floor canter to the lower side. It was a private sale and the owner, a well-known architect with two blond little daughters and a vivacious wife. The goat was tethered to a stake and eating the vegetation of derelict land between the house and the harbour. In the middle of the ground floor it had a slow combustion cast iron wood heater with a galvanised chimney going up through the roof. As an extra bonus it could also include a huge boulder that was about ten metres by thirty metres long, and could be leased from the local council. This boulder would extend our property to the next street corner giving us the right for intruders to be excluded.

We immediately went to the bank to try and get a mortgage. The manager promised an inspection and after a week he got back to us. 'Look, Gerard mate,' he said, 'you are buying a glorified shed. Are you sure you want to go through with it?' Our deposit was sixty percent, so the bank had little option but to approve of the loan. The 'shed,' after six weeks or so, became ours. It was our 'dream of own house on own block' come true. The morning sun would come up over the harbour bridge and then reflect on the hardwood timber flooring. Looking against the light, the water was sparkling and shimmering. Boats and ferries busying themselves, with large merchant ships reversing engines before berthing, making the landmass and our house rattle and shake. Sydney still was an industrial harbour and full of life. The derelict land adjacent and in front of the cottage facing the harbour was ideal for throwing in a fishing line. Many did so, especially during weekends. Our little family thrived as did the business. In the meantime, I kept on with my art and painted many pictures. At one stage we had nude life drawing classes. Our friends would sometimes strip off and allow themselves to be drawn in charcoal. Many early and adventurous couples decided to also buy those cheap places in Balmain, do them up and restore them to former glory. Of course, working class cottages that were small and modest could hardly become 'former glory mansions', and some of the results were far from modest and ruined many of them. Extensions and extra storeys on top of former two bedroom cottage on small parcels of land ended up ugly and bloated. The flexing of moneyed people did not enhance the area in later years, either. The bath in the middle of the living area was eventually screened off. Adjacent to the bath we had a second hand washing machine with the draining of rinsing water done by lowering the hose to the outside and then sucking on it to encourage the flow. Nowadays, it could be seen as a bit primitive, but to have a washing machine that did everything except pumping out the water, that defect was seen as a minor dysfunction. The cottage itself, with its open sunny feeling, could only be improved upon by bits of furniture that we mainly scrounged around for in second hand shops, St Vinnie's etc. It was shielded from the street by a very high timber fence that the previous architect owner had put up. It was so high that you could not even jump up to get a hold and climb over it. Some friends that had lived in Indonesia remarked it reminded them of a brothel that the Japanese were running during the occupation. No doubt, if it would have been possible to have had a look inside during the nude drawing lessons that the brothel conclusion could have been drawn as well.

The Good Years of Bra Burnings and Baby-Sitting.

We moved from Kings Cross to our house in Balmain with all our belongings in the back of our Ford Zephyr utility. We had bought this utility from Pacific Auction car sales on Parramatta Road after arrival in Australia. They had a slogan, 'Pacific is Terrific'. They were indeed. You put your bid on the car of your choice that was being driven in front of a podium where a man with a booming voice would announce the cars to be auctioned to the highest bidder. It was fast moving. The buyers were supposed to check the vehicles beforehand. No guarantee was given to roadworthiness. It wasn't unusual for a car refusing to start, in which case the car was pushed by well-muscled helpers or sometimes even the buyers with much laughter and shouts of, 'Who wants this bomb?' Helvi came with me and thought it hugely entertaining. I had always bought my cars there and would go and buy another one if the present car was on its last leg. However, I never had a car on three wheels and bricks like those Dutch Friends had in the timber yard after our family's arrival in 1956, together with a large dog on three legs chasing huge and very fast rats (on four legs). (Sometime later, I worked in a factory where the owner was suspected of having just one leg because there was a strange creaking sound escaping from his trousers when he was walking.)

The Ford Zephyr utility was, however, the car which I had fantasised so much about back in Holland. Remember how our Dutch friends had written they bought a car that was sometimes a sedan and at other times a truck. I thought then it was a modern American invention whereby with the push of a button a car would morph from one model into the next.

Of course, in the meantime, I had learnt the harsh reality that truth and fantasy are bad bedfellows and rarely did the twain meet. In our apartment at Kanimbla Hall in Kings Cross we had a seat made and some bookshelves. We bought a long piece of hard rubber which we had covered with a nice deep wine-red coloured piece of strong material bought from Artes Studio at Sydney's George Street. The rubber was cut to size from a Clark Rubber shop. Clark Rubber was the place for young couples to get cheap furnishings together with a good range of hiking boots and camping gear, including cast iron camp stoves that used to get suspended from a tripod when camping in which to cook potatoes or make a stew. It just took one day to move from our apartment in Kings Cross to Balmain. Diligent (or foolhardy) readers would have learnt that by that time we had two lovely daughters. A newspaper article appeared whereby a Mum from Balmain had set up play groups for Mums and pre-school toddlers. This was really a fantastic initiative. It was simple. On given days, Mums and young children would meet at a local playground, join each other and the children who would play around on the slippery dips, the round-a-bout and sandpit. The Mums would get to know each other and the children. I am not sure, but I think that government or private pre-schools for toddlers below aged four years had as yet not been invented. The play groups were hugely successful, and soon after, a babysitting group was formed. It worked on a point system. Each hour of babysitting for someone would earn a plus point. A minus point would be deducted if own child was baby-sat. It was expected that plus and minus points would balance out within a reasonable time-frame.

Those with good memories would know that, thanks to Germaine Greer, the bra was more and more seen as a fashion article of enslavement, a tool to keep them (breasts) propped up, purely for the sake of looks and salivating males. It went further, and it was suggested they were designed together with girdles and make-up as a ploy to keep women shackled to the kitchen sink and nappy buckets. It was therefore also suggested to ditch the bra and if a droop resulted, be proud and walk tall. Together with ditching the bra, radical lesbianism was embraced. I never witnessed any bra burning or rampaging lesbians but do remember going to a party held at a professor of philosophy house who insisted all women hang their bras on the door knob before allowed in. They all did, and it was one of the more memorable parties in Balmain.

I have been credited in Balmain, still even today, of having lifted the ban, not on bras, but on men not being allowed to babysit. The stranglehold of some women on insisting only women would be allowed to babysit was broken when in all innocence I turned up one evening. A nervous Mum made a hurried telephone call to the secretary and after a while it was decided I could baby sit. The year was 1973. With my Dutch and Helvi's heritage I never even thought that it was solely the domain of women in our home countries to sit on babies. Anyway, it was different then in Australia. From the early seventies, 1973 to be precise, men were allowed to babysit at each other's houses. It was a male revolution on par with bra burning. You can thank Gerard for this! It was odd that some women felt emancipated by going bra-less and yet thought that it was a bit dodgy for male friends to do babysitting. It should be written up in our history books, or at least on Wikipedia.

Winter in America, Children's Library and Veggie Co-op.

The way things are going in this auto-biography, it will run into a literary cinemascope version of 'Days of our Lives,' with the Hammond organ belting out a circular and never ending tune. The cheek of thinking that my life is any better or more important or interesting than that of any Joe Blow! I shall just continue because I enjoy this writing and remembering very much. And if there is a blow-out of too many words, well...just skip a few pages... or start at the end, and work towards the middle. Even if it relieves insomnia for a single night for just one single person, I'll be a happy man.

Apart from the baby-sitting club, another community enterprise was the veggie co-op which also started to sprout up in the various communities of inner Sydney suburbs. I am not sure anymore if this came about during our stay at Gertrude's Cottage between 1969 and 1973 or after our stay in Holland and subsequent return in 1976. In any case, a group of people decided to fork out ten dollars each week towards a group to buy fruit and vegetables at the Flemington wholesale fruit and veggie markets at Homebush. It was a huge market covering a very large area where all the fruit and veggie shops would get their produce at wholesale prices. It also had several cafeteria where the buyers could get breakfast and coffee, smoke a cigarette. Many fruit and veggie shops were run by Italians and Greeks. Food and coffees were as necessary as the apples, kale and celery which they filled their trucks up with. The market opened up at five am. You can imagine how early the growers had to get up and prepare their stalls? Farming is tough! It was a hectic few hours and the men, and many women too, would be ravenous by seven am. The market, as all markets do, also had great atmosphere, and laughter was everywhere. Of interest was my market shopping partner Jimmy Stewart. He was Irish. He loved a good yarn and food. He looked somewhat like a juvenile Oscar Wilde. He had dark hair hanging over his face, and a large stomach. After our shopping of many boxes of fruit and veggies, we would visit the cafeteria, enjoy bacon and eggs, coffee and a cigarette. He loved women and they generously reciprocated, yet he was never good marriage material. His income sporadic and swallowed up by international phone calls to entrepreneurial music and record companies. He generally managed to get me to buy cigarettes and pay for the bacon and eggs. But, he was terrific company, always whistling and singing. A cheerful soul. A great friend. He was a writer of music, popular music, and would let nothing stand in the way of doing that. Sadly, it did not bring in a regular income. Women were attracted to him often in order to find out that a future including a cosy and secure family-life would be hazardous at best and reckless at worst. That's how so often, and so sadly, love gets lost. The combination of income with a mutual everlasting and reasonable attraction is so desired, and yet so rarely achieved. Money so often the banana skin on the doorstep of many relationships. Indeed, even with plenty of money things can get perilous.

While we drove to the markets and back he used to hum a song that really hit the world soon after. It was 'Winter in America'. It had a line that included the 'Frangipani'. 'The harbour's misty in the morning, love, oh how I miss December / the Frangipani opens up to kiss the salty air.' Ashdown's lament to 'Leave Love Enough Alone' has become one of the great Australian standards. It was Jimmy Stewart's creation and he would often sing it while driving to Flemington markets...At the same time of the weekly boxes of fruit and veggies, another group also brought to fruition was a Children's library. Another community effort. The retired chief Commonwealth librarian, Larry Lake, was the main person behind this idea. The National Trust had given the use of the Balmain Lock-up to a group that called themselves, 'The Balmain

Association.' The 'Lock-up' or 'Watch House' was busy locking up drunks and vagabonds during the heydays of Balmain still working as a Stevedoring and Waterfront suburb. There were lots of maritime associated industries, and that is what attracted many new people to the area when that ceded to exist. During earlier times and at night the local constable would have been busy locking up inebriated sailors or others that liked to frequent so many pubs, it was difficult to find normal houses in between. I believe Balmain had over sixty pubs at one stage. The evenings used to be thick with coarse oaths renting the smoky air with rank vomit along the blue-stone cobbled noisy streets. It frightened the horses at times.

A group including myself spent many evenings getting this library working. There were fundraisings and book coverings, cataloguing and getting shelving to fit into one of the lock-up cells. It had a heavy steel door and sliding locking mechanism. Those poor drunks! The children that used to visit the cell library afterwards loved it. Those were the days. It did not just only include occasional bra removals. It was a thriving community with baby-sitting clubs, veggie co-ops, and a community run children's library.

The Good Years, 1966-1973.

With the birth of our two daughters, life in Gertrude's Cottage was enjoyed along a steady forward path. I remember it mainly as a very bright sunny yellow reflection on the timber floor with a shimmering expanse of water in the distance. A few years of uninterrupted family bliss. I had my own business. The painting of pictures was done in between shooting out to deliver material or organise meetings with builders, clerk of works, or quoting for new contracts. I can remember painting mainly on the floor. Most of my work was entered into municipal competitions and I had a list of dates and places of when and where to send the paintings. I do remember that the size of the paintings became larger and larger perhaps in tandem with the growing of our little family. An expression of exuberance? The paintings also became braver.

https://en.wikipedia.org/wiki/Desiderius_Orban

It was one of those inexplicable fates of lucky circumstance that I met a Hungarian painter who taught art in the very heart of Sydney. It was at Sydney's Rocks, just metres away from the Harbour Bridge. His name was Desiderius Orban. He had established himself as a modern and successful painter. He had also published a book on art, and was a well-known teacher. He did not really teach in the sense that he showed you a skill or technique. He encouraged rather than taught, and very much pushed the students in expressing whatever was in them. He did not care if you painted with a brush, a stick or your fingers. He was already very old, but even so, lived on forever. Some people when getting old seem to get a new burst of life when already well past the age when most people are happy to take a permanent rest in the urn or the reserved plot of no return. He died aged one hundred and one years old.

One artist that seems to deny or defy the welcoming (but icy embrace) of the dearly departed so far, is John Olsen. Readers might remember I took art lessons at a much earlier time from the Mary White School of art where he and Robert Klippel were doing some teaching. This was before my marriage whilst still living at home. Both teachers were free spirits and used to go to the local pub and imbibe a couple, only to return rather jovial and praising all students no matter what they had cobbled together.

https://en.wikipedia.org/wiki/John_Olsen_(artist)
https://en.wikipedia.org/wiki/Robert_Klippel

John Olsen is still alive today (30/7/2015) and one of the only too rare an instance where his paintings are selling for millions and the artist able to enjoy it. How Vincent would turn is his grave? With the continuation of entering my paintings in competition, it would be outside the law of averages, if sooner or later, I would not hit the jackpot. Hitting the jackpot might be a bit exaggerated seeing the prices were rather within the limits of the Shire's income forever struggling with keeping rates low. It was more of a way to climb the ladder to getting known, and even more important, able to sell the work. I did win a couple of prices. I had a painting accepted and hung in the Art Gallery of New South Wales. The painting was named 'Billabong.'

http://www.artgallery.nsw.gov.au/prizes/wynne/1972/2 4292/ I was not only happy but well hung as well.

It was also in that year that Helvi visited her family in Finland with both our daughters. I stayed behind to continue the decorating business. I had promised to look after the eldest daughter's teddy bear by giving it porridge. The KLM flight included a photo taken of Helvi carrying the youngest in the Papoose which at the time was a novel way of traveling with very young children. This photo went worldwide in the KLM's magazine. It was a great shot, and I wish I could find it. Alas, it is 'somewhere' in our apartment but hidden in either boxes, linen-drawers or even albums. Somewhere!

Billabong.

Life Drawing With the Fondue.

"The etymology of the word *billabong* is disputed. The word is most likely derived from the Wiradjuri term *bilabaŋ*, which means "a watercourse that runs only after rain" and is derived from *bila*, meaning "river", and possibly *bong* or *bung*, meaning "dead". One source, however, claims that the term is of Scottish Gaelic origin. Billabongs attained significance as they held water longer than parts of rivers and it was therefore important for people to name these areas."

Gaelic or aboriginal, I'll settle for the latter, and painted accordingly in the ochre, chrome yellow, sienna colouring and avoided any kilt hues.

The above painting, 'Billabong', must have got the nod of approval by the panel of judges and was hung in the NSW Gallery in 1972. The seventies was a period, not only of veggie co-ops, baby-sitting clubs and going bra-less, it was also a period of enormous cultural change in Australia. It all started in the late sixties and had its origin in a couple of cafes around the Cross in Sydney. I think Frank Morehouse, an Australian writer, was savvy to this, and even wrote a book called, 'Days of Wine and Rage.' Up till the late sixties, the Nescafe instant coffee was the preferred brown drink. For many years, TV advertisements used to swear each cup had 43 beans of 'real coffee', implying that there were coffees around that were not 'real', conveniently forgetting that Nescafe instant coffee is as far removed from being real coffee than 'tasty cheese' is from being an honest cheese. Most readers of this blog would know my stand on 'tasty cheese'! Towards the end of the sixties, a coffee lounge opened up named 'Reggios' at the corner of Crown street and near Chapel Street, Sydney. Not only was it one of the first 'real' coffee lounges to open, it was also selling the best coffee in town, and it was 'real' coffee percolated from 'real' beans. Reggio's was frequented by a lot of Italians. Many were migrants from boats such as Roma and Sydney. Most were single. If one looked carefully it was noticed that many looked somewhat doe-eyed. The tragedy of a shortage of available women was expressed in their eyes after they lifted their faces from the empty coffee cups, and looked into mine. I understood their plight.

A few girls of the night soon cottoned onto this Mediterranean loneliness, and for a modest sum would allow some relief to the forlorn of Messina or Napoli. It wasn't the kind of love those men sought but it was better than nothing. The coffee afterwards helped. But it was a love so bitter and not helped by the dusty train journey home afterwards to their even lonelier beds and petunia laced suburbs. Soon, more coffee lounges followed. Today, it has become a mile long stretch of coffee lounges, and cafés, catering for the well-heeled, the property developers, the gangsters, toy boys, and their well coiffured owners. Many are sitting under the striped awnings together with their barristers or Labor Ministers. All are wildly gesticulating and doing their sipping. Of course, there is so much more to coffee now.

There is a bewilderingly long list of different coffees available. It frightens me, as I have long ago given up in remembering the latest of this or that. We still ask for a simple 'latte'. Does anyone in our age group ask for a macchiato coffee? I doubt it. What is it?

In between running a business we also found time to do life drawing and have fondue parties. The fondue set would come down from the top cupboard, and with the help of a little dish with methylated spirits, we would cook bits of raw meat in a container with oil which was heated by the methylated spirits. The meat was held at the end of steel prongs. The fad lasted for a few years together with exercise bikes. I noticed there has been an upsurge of exercise machinery. Some look as if they are ready to go on an outer space journey. So massive, I wonder if they can double as a diesel truck or prime mover or a good metal turning lathe. Would it not be better to go for a walk, or has that become too dangerous with pensioner stalking the streets? In any case, society had progressed and nothing was not tried and experimented with. It came about that some would eagerly strip off for a spontaneous life drawing session all inside our Gertrude cottage. Of course, that is finished. Can one imagine the horror of stripping off now? There would be a stampede out of Gertrude's Cottage or a call to the police, even an ambulance!

Those were the days.

A Salaried Artist in 1973.

Back in the early seventies, I read a Dutch magazine featuring a Mayor of a small Dutch town. In it, he spoke about artists, and how he wanted to encourage the arts to flourish in his municipality. Also, in the same magazine was mentioned a Government initiative many years before in making this happen. It was very simple, really. Artists would be paid a basic salary, the same as most workers. It was argued that the making of art was as valid as making bread or driving a train. Art was as necessary and equally esteemed as a bicycle. Indeed, art was the very bicycle of the spirit and soul. Was it Marcel Duchamp who pointed that out? It was decided that in exchange for their production of art, the maker or creator of this art would be paid a salary which would enable him to live with comfort, and with dignity. It seemed so pragmatic and so utterly Dutch. The article struck me as a lightning bolt from the sky. I became feverishly emboldened. I promptly wrote to this Mayor in which I greatly appreciated his aim in encouraging creative work in Holland. At the same time I made enquiries on how the system of creating art in exchange for a salary worked. While in Australia, the combination of running a business as well as doing art worked reasonably well, it wasn't as ideal as it could be. The idea of a salaried artist germinated into fertile soil. I could not let go of the idea. At the same time, I felt a rekindling of a kind and benevolent Holland. An artistic Dutch Nirvana! I would be regaining my home-country. It grew stronger by the day. Gone were the memories of daily rain and howling storms. I pushed aside those earlier memories visiting my friends who put on the TV within minutes of my arrival. Instead, a welcoming home to this lost Dutch prodigal son from Australia emerged like a fata morgana strangely affixed amongst an aurora in a Nordic sky. Of course, it also blew out of all proportions. I was running a head of foaming steam.

I received a letter back from this Mayor advising me to contact him if and when we would arrive. I still had the Dutch nationality, and right from the beginning, our stay in Australia was decided it would be temporary. It was envisaged we somehow would get a house (hut) made of solid pine in a Finnish forest. Helvi would teach, and I would paint. Life would be simple and joyous. The Mayor's article, and the Dutch artist salary made us decide to do the simple and joyous in Holland instead. Please consider that we were young and idealistic. It was the only way to be.

With ageing might come experiences that wilts idealism, blows the autumnal leaves, sometimes even icy blasts? Of course, to keep making art that doesn't give an income is the slippery slope that bedevils many. The Dutch Government artist's support whereby the art was bought for a monthly salary seemed so good. Manna from heaven. It was so popular many overseas artists also flocked to Holland. The art was used to decorate the walls, floors or gardens of public buildings. Jails, hospitals, parliament buildings, schools, libraries, child care, municipality town-halls, swimming pools, Law

Courts, Family Divorce courts... you name it, all were flooded with art works. When those public buildings became saturated with paintings, ceramics, wall hangings, sculptures, a law was passed named 'The Percentage in Art Acquisition.' It forced all large planned private buildings to spend a percentage of the total building costs on buying creative works to decorate the new building. It was a boon that created an enormous output of art surpassing the (over) production of the world's largest EU butter mountain a few years later. Of course, it went without saying that libraries started lending art works as well. People would take a painting home for a few weeks and swap for another one.

In 1973, we sold Gertrude's Cottage, packed as many suitcases we could take on the plane, and after landing at Holland's Schiphol, rented a car. We slept one night in a hotel near the airport. Next day, after breakfast of ham and cheese rolls with coffee, we drove north to the small town and the Mayor. He was extremely helpful, and indeed knew a farmer who had just moved into a new farm house who was willing to let us rent the old farm-house. He had it all arranged for us. How glorious. We had packed air mattresses for the five of us. (That's right, between Helvi on holiday in Finland in 1972, with our two daughters and her return to Balmain, we had a third baby, a glorious boy this time.) The second night we slept on air mattresses on the floor of the old farm, quite chuffed that all had turned out so reasonably well. It was a lovely spring and sunny. That helped a lot.

The Artist as Employee and Making New Antique Clocks.

The first weeks were spent getting good bedding and turning the heating on. It was early May and still surprisingly cold. We enrolled both our daughters in the local kindergarten school. Our son stayed home as he was still a baby. Soon after we bought a VW Kombi bus. The VW bus popularity was a world-wide phenomenon. There was an unwritten universal law that drivers of those VW buses would dip their headlights while passing each other on the road. Most often those drivers were anti-war, anti-plastic but pro-whales. Both sexes grew long hair, smoked bongs, drank cheap red wine, and listened to Simon and Garfunkel's, 'Bridge over Troubled Water'. We also had to establish our citizenship and get enrolled into all the different levels of the Dutch bureaucracy which is fairly complicated but generous. Child endowment, unemployment relief, all sorts of taxation requirements, getting banking accounts fixed. All went reasonably smooth, and when things had settled I enrolled myself at an employment office seeking work as an 'artist'. Much to my surprise, within a few days I was notified about a vacancy for an artist. An artist skilled in landscape techniques. It was about a twenty minute drive from where we were living. I was so intrigued. Can you believe this?

I turned up for the interview at a factory that made imitation grandfather clocks. Those clocks were selling like hot cakes, exported worldwide, especially the 'Friesian stand-up clock' with a swinging pendulum and hand painted clock dial. All had to be genuinely hand painted. This is where the job of the artist came in, specifically my skill as the artist landscape or sky/sea scape specialist. If possible, it would be best if the clock dials were painted in a genuine style. A kind of mixture between a Hobbema and Vermeer would do nicely.

I felt that it might be well worth the experience. After whipping out a quick little sample of a wind-mill and some sea-gulls, I was given the job. From what I could see on some of the clocks with hand-painted dials, the previous painter wasn't really skilled in faking an old master in any genre. The factory making the clocks was actually part of a much larger consortium doing all sorts of things including exporting tulips to America. I was in good hands. The salary was not bad either. Remember how I had taken lessons from Ronald Peters at the Parramatta ambulance hall in the late fifties early sixties in painting landscapes with a receding sky and dappled effects on gum tree trunks? Well, all this was now coming to fruition at the clock factory. Those clocks were really amazing. The actual body of the grandfather clock was made from something that was poured in a mould. When taken out of the mould a brown stain was sprayed over it and, lo and behold, it looked like genuine oak. The actual grain of the oak was part of the mould. Amazing fake that could not be improved upon. Of course, today everything is fake. Reading only yesterday on a bottle of maple syrup at Aldi in small lettering, 'Maple flavoured.'

At the same time as my clock dial painting career took off, we also bought an original Dutch farm house with a soaring upwards, part-tiled and part thatched roof, typical of that Northern area. Many traditional Old Dutch farms had both people and cows living inside during winter under the same roof. Hay that was cut during summer was stored inside together with cows and people. One reason for those high roofs was to stack the hay. It was all very cosy, intimate and, above all in winter, nice and warm. The cows heated the place up better than central heating ever could. Of course, we did not keep cows in our bedroom, and did have central heating installed. The clock dial painting went very well. The management was very happy. A lot depended on the attractiveness of the clock face. They were bought solely on their looks. The seagulls especially were very real. The manager said, 'They seem to follow me around the room.' I was emboldened to such a degree I managed to do the production of clock dial painting at home on the farm. Once a week I would drive over and hand the works of art in and pick up a box of blank clock faces in return. As long as I did about fifty dials a week, all would be happy. I had achieved a fairly relaxed way of earning a salary, and as yet had no need to apply for the Government artist salary. That was yet to come!

Of course, the clocks were super kitsch, and some might query the moral fibre of someone happily doing that, but...who was I to not experience the life of a paid artist. Did not Jan Steen (1626-1679) run a tavern, have nine children and two wives. What about Pieter Brueghel before (1525-1569), with his rejected 'The Blind Leading the Blind?' There is hope for all Dutchmen and women! We all make the best of circumstance.

Repetition Always Results In Ennui.

It seems that repetition is always present no matter where or how we live. I find myself queuing at the supermarket almost daily. I still hold out hope for something to happen there. It never does. I scan other peoples' shopping lists and so wish for some answers. I can see by the shoppers' eyes, they too want something more than the repetitiousness of life. A kind of unexpected surprise. The cashiers put a positive spin on things. They were told to ask about the wellbeing of the shopper. 'How are you?' And I answer, 'Great, thank you.' I encourage and nurture the repeating of a stupefying routine. We are all in cahoots. Yet, the sun is shining and the croissants are on special. Three for $1.99.

Was it therefore inevitable that the painting of clock dials would come to an end sooner than anticipated? Even the move to another farm on the East of Holland could only hold off the end of my clock painting career for just a while. My tolerance for routine I never mastered. Some people thrive on knowing exactly what to expect next day, next year, next decade, and get nervous when they don't. Of course, we all accept some routine. We shop and pay bills. We fill the car with petrol and stare at the browser with keen intent. At the super market I play a silly game with Helvi, and tell her the amount that our shopping will come to. I just scan all the goods on the conveyer belt and make a guess. I tell Helvi and the cashier the amount before the scanning takes place. Helvi rolls her eyes. When I get close, it makes my morning and I smile. It helps to pass the time! The cashier gives a smile, too.

One morning when I had set up the clock dials all in a row on the worktable, I could not get to paint another seagull. Helvi and I had done at least six months of clock faces at fifty a week. That is at least twelve hundred clock faces, and at roughly four seagulls a piece, amounted to four thousand eight hundred fucking seagulls, give or take a few. (I had reduced seagulls of late. A clear sign that the end was nigh.) I packed the box of dials, and drove back to the clock factory to give notice. I was jubilant, and had put on the car radio. The manager understood. He, too, suffered the same lethargy, and had a large family. He took satisfaction from being a good provider, putting food on the table. He also used to go fishing on the weekends. 'It brings me peace and quiet,' he said, smiling. Lots of Dutch people go fishing and also like doing cross-word puzzles. It helps, and makes life bearable.

We are all so brave.

The Artist as Teacher.

After the adieu to the imitation Dutch Grandfather Clock period with the last box of painted clock dials being dropped off at the imitation clock factory, I did finally apply for the 'Dutch Artist' salary. I filled in forms with proof of my birth, and educational levels. My quantity surveying qualification could easily throw this whole undertaking askew. I had to tread carefully! It was something to ponder. What about if the recommendation came back suggesting I should work in an office calculating bills of quantities instead of doing art? I knew the Dutch bureaucracy might like art but they also had a very practical side to their culture. They could easily tell me to get a real job. I had nightmares of having left Gertrude Cottage in Australia, traveling to Holland itching to paint full time AND finally have an income, only to end up wearing a suit to an office and sadly having to pour over bills of quantities, working out quantities for cement or sewer pipes for the latest and world's best recycling plant.

On the other hand, I did have proof with the success of being well 'hung' at the NSW State Gallery and a couple of prizes at Australian Municipal competitions. Through a friend, I had also managed to show some of my work at a gallery in Japan's Kyoto. I wasn't totally unprepared. Even so, I decided sagely to remain mum about my quantity surveying qualification, my previous bank experiences, and my prowess in the decorating business with the buff coloured letterheads and matching envelopes.

Was I dishonest and not somewhat duplicitous? Many artists do other jobs, provide for a family and do their art? Why even worry about that? Wasn't it always a kind of wild-haired bohemian wearing a beret at a rakish angle that created? If it became too hard he would simply disregard spouses and crying babies. He, and sometimes a she, would walk out, satchel, easel, and pallet on shoulder, whistling in the wind, going up and beyond hill, gone forever. New daisies and fragrant meadows were beckoning and to be explored! Many 'real artists' would leave a trail of relationship disasters with endlessly and chaotically dividing children of many sexes. Desperate love affairs were obligatory in most that claim to possess creative powers. Leaving spouses was the very essence and proof of creative forces at work. History is full of the wrath of partners betrayed. Daggers were raised and many artists' lives ended painfully, their canvasses slashed. Today, the Family Court sorts it all out, but it costs an arm and a leg just the same as before with spouse and marriage or the knife. Of course, the 'real artist' does not care. He continues creating, whistling.

Alas, I loved Helvi and my family dearly. I applied for this salary that would give me freedom to paint my pictures. I filled in the forms, submitted some of my work. I was asked to wait in a large hallway with other applicants. Public servants were shuffling around while lifts carried up the works that had been submitted. The hallway resembled a doctor's waiting room. Nervous looking artists. Some had berets, others wore important beards or had paint smeared on their hands and clothing. You wondered what discussions were taking place in the art judges' room. I just hoped they would not get the paintings mixed up. The man who accepted my paintings did look askance, and somewhat bored. I suppose if one did that for a job, it might not be all that different from painting seagulls. Would he go home to his partner and regale about the paintings or sculptures and ceramics he had seen that day. I mean, day in day out? I did hear some laughter coming out of the room. Were they ridiculing some of the work? I had a peek at one artist's paintings and they were all of large oysters. He was obviously taken by the sea and its creative forces. Why not? An oyster is such a magnificent work on its own.

At the end of it all, we were asked to take our work back. We would be told by letter. It took a few nail biting weeks yet.

The Commission for a Mural and Teaching Adults.

The good news came as predicted within a few weeks. Just when some other, even better tiding knocked on our barn's door. The area where we had bought our second farm was near a village that was set and artificially kept in the eighteen hundreds. It is called Orvelte and is a museum village. Some of the people living there were artists on the Government salary but, as they were given an old farm-house as well as a salary, also expected to produce art sympathetic to the bygone era of horse-carts, peat cutting, thatching, smithing of horse shoes, thrashing of hay and each other. Each Saturday afternoon there would be a village dance which tourists in strange shorts would photograph with large cameras, and even larger lenses.

Our daughters, Susanna and Natasha, being enrolled in the local school (their second Dutch school) quickly made friends. Both started to speak fluent Dutch at an astonishing speed. Through their friends, we met some parents, including a couple that lived in Orvelte who made pottery. The pottery was in keeping with this historic village. Good solid salt-glazed stoneware. We bought a set of cups and saucers, a bulky vase, wine goblets and large serving dish. None have broken so far. The potter and his wife made a living from the potter's wheel and also enjoyed the Government Artist salary. It turned out he was as fed up with his conveyer belt production of stone pottery as I was with the previous clock dials with seagulls in endless flight.

Our very Old Saxon Farm house in Holland with Helvi and our three children.

The potter and his wife soon joined our friendship with another couple. This time the husband claimed to be a sculptor. He even managed to get the local shire to put up signage along the village roads pointing to his house with studio. When I visited him, after introduction, I asked if he would be so kind as to show me some of his work, and he obliged. He showed me a glass case with a lid, behind in which he kept some drawings of work he had done at The Art Academy years before. And that was that! Not a single work, not even a block of stone or lump of clay lying about. He normally charged an entrance fee to tourists to see his drawings inside this glass case with a lid. When he spotted my Kombi he quickly asked if I would be so kind as to pick up a wardrobe somewhere. I did. Helvi wasn't impressed. But I explained he did not charge me to look at his drawings. Even so, we needed friends, and we invited them for an afternoon. He ate all of our peanuts. He must have been so hungry. His hand kept throwing those nuts back into his tilted upward mouth. It is strange how those memories keep sticking. I mean, we did not mind the peanut frenzy, but were just somewhat surprised. Heaven knows what others make of us? 'Gerard is really weird and strange,' they could well whisper behind closed doors!

did love in

The commissioned mural at Westerbork School.

Another couple we tried to befriend included a printmaker. I knocked on his door. He just poked his throbbing red face through a window and asked what I wanted. I explained we were from Australia seeking friendship. 'I am an artist, too,' I said bravely, while nodding affirmatively and somewhat conspiratorially. 'Oh,' he said without hesitation, 'I am having a fight with my wife. I can't see you.' He slammed the window shut. Marital fights in Holland are just as prevalent as anywhere. Just because they ride bikes, eat herrings and live abstemious lives doesn't mean they don't suffer marital whiplash at times. It is universal. We did keep a few couples as friends, including the potter couple of stone-ware. He worked as a part-time teacher and informed me the school for adult education was looking for a teacher in the creative arts, especially painting and drawing. I got the job. This was the other good news I was alluding to at the beginning of this piece. But that wasn't the end of happy and happier! I won a commission to make a mural for a yet to be built school in the small town where my daughters attended school. This town is named Westerbork. It all came good. Sorry for the black and white photo. It was a triptych.

The Pregnant Shetland and a Foal.

With roughly more than seven decades between the beginning and now, one has to allow for some discrepancies on these memories. Memories change and could at times be unreliable. The order and dates might not be exact but the events mainly true. One might also have to allow that the events are somewhat embellished to make them more readable or perhaps even enjoyable. A French polished table doesn't make it less or more of a table if presented in raw oak. The specimen of my life is not any different from the multitudes of other lives. It is also not any more unique in its minutia than those other lives of this world. I write what I feel was important. But the nature of writing an autobiography or memoirs implies a certain amount of egoism. I do it to continue with my life as I have in the past. Keep myself off the street. I enjoy the confessional part of it, but also realize it is a race against time with the inevitability of those final last words that befall all of us. The pole vaulting days are over, but writing about it makes solid the past. A kind of coagulation of a mishmash of memories rusted reddish-brown onto the years gone by. The words as yet not said do remain knocking.

The school that our daughters went to was about a ten minute bicycle ride along a sweet little country lane into the small town. Both used to come home for lunch, and go off again for afternoon lessons. At no stage did we even contemplate that there were dangers of traffic or bad people prowling about. Children getting to school on their own was the norm. At least in The Netherlands. It was idyllic. Even in the country, no distance seemed beyond a ride on a bicycle. No safety helmets were worn either. All was safe, and there were bicycle paths separating riders from cars. We had sheep, chickens and a pregnant Shetland pony. What more could one ask for?

One winter morning, there was a furious tapping on our bedroom window. Our bedroom was at the front of the farm overlooking the meadow in which the sheep and pony grazed. It was our neighbour. He was a serious farmer, unlike us. 'You have a foal, Gerard. Get up, and hang the afterbirth,' he said. Of course it wasn't in those words. The dialect in the area we lived in was as unlike Dutch as Scottish is from English, or Welsh from Irish. Is there some unwritten law that men respond to tapping on bedroom windows, and not the female? In any case, it had snowed outside. Our bed was warm. Even so, I did admire and liked our neighbour's care for our pony. He had already told us it looked she might un-pack at any moment. I got out of bed, and went outside just wearing slippers with a morning coat. Indeed, there was this trembling but lovely little foal, barely able to stand up to take its first suckle.

I don't know why an afterbirth had to be hung up from a tree away from ground-hugging predators such as a canny fox, wolf or bear. It was a tradition steeped in folklore and we apparently had chosen our farm in a village that were the harbingers and last owners of some very ancient habits which must not be disregarded. We, after all, were living here as strangers, and really almost imposters more than traditional owners, and had to tread carefully with respect to keeping their traditions. I stumbled about, found the afterbirth, and flung it over the large elm next to the farm house. Both Mum and baby Shetland were doing fine. Our neighbours were happy too.

Teaching and the Obstinate Shetland pony.

We all know that Shetland ponies are escape artists. When you see them looking down, they are actually thinking. 'How the hell can I get out of this joint?' Our Shetland was a Houdini. I would get a phone call: 'Hey Gerard, your horse is in town.' I would jump on my bike with the lead in hand. I would cycle back, Shetland on rope. Give her a stern talking to and put her back in with the sheep and chickens. I would again fix the wire fence, but also knew she would soon figure a way out again. When the foal was born she stopped escaping. There are so many memories fondly embedded in that period that I am at risk of never finishing what I set out to do. The aim is to meander from the beginning of my family's migration in 1956 till my present state of blissful dotage. Still, words at times seem to have a will of their own, like a Shetland, and lead to unexpected and totally arbitrary directions. My apologies.

The job of teaching came about through a friend named Jan Muller who was doing the salt glazed pottery and lived in the museum village of Orvelte, and who was teaching at a college for adults. After a short interview, I started teaching at the same college. That was the best time of our stay in Holland. The first day of teaching was somewhat nerve wrecking. Who was I to teach anything? I wasn't taught anything. Failed even the Phyllis Bates 'Academy of Dance' of Foxtrot and the Rumba. And that was with the dance steps painted on the floor! Of course, I had a good grounding from Desiderius Orban, the Hungarian master teacher at The Rocks in Sydney. He lived till 101 years. At the time we lived in Holland, I was still in contact with him. Fear is what prevents many from employing what we are all born with. The ability to express and give form to some creativity, no matter how humble or grandiose. The first lesson, if I remember correctly, was to try and get all the adults to put charcoal or pencil to paper. Now, if you had a group of toddlers, they would instantly without exception start to doodle furiously and with great joy! Not so with many adults. It is sad. They had lost this spontaneity and joy. Many would as a first option say, 'I can't draw.' They say that before any attempt was made to put a single dot on the paper. How do you know? You don't know if you don't try! 'Go on, put the charcoal on the paper just draw a line or just a single dot!'

My first day was to try and make the students approach the paper without fear. Somehow, the enthusiasm of the toddler had to be regained. That is what my aim of teacher was. I could not teach just skill or things like shading or making portrait eyes follow you around the room or photo-like images of apples or strawberries so real that the paper or canvas was almost bitten into by the ambitious but starving student while wearing a beret and paint spackled jeans.

The End of the Dutch Affair.

While the three years in Holland are worthy of a book-tome on its own, I have to move on. Time is of the essence. Having arrived at seventy-five since the seventh of August this year, and with at least another forty years to record, I must move on from the nineteen-seventies. A derailment is a possibility! Still, I must remain sanguine and take heart from the statistics that tell me there is an eighty percent chance of turning eighty-five for those that are in good health at seventy-five. However, the odds of turning ninety-five at eighty-five years of age are less cheerful.

A few art shows followed the primary school triptych commission. Here and there paintings were sold, and generally things were steaming along nicely. Our three children were growing fast, but not so fast that driving around in the Kombi wasn't at times a somewhat difficult and testing task. Young children on long car trips is a job too far. Who would not be bored sitting confined in a metal box on rotating rubber wheels? Instead of long drives, we set up tents in the paddocks together with sheep and Shetlands. It was a blessing. The kids loved it, and with two tents they could swap around if there were disagreements about which teddy to sleep with or who had pinched an extra biscuit.

My brother Frank, with his long suffering chronic schizophrenia, was finally repatriated and taken back to Holland in 1975. Australia doesn't serve the disadvantaged well. It had been a hell. In bewildered desperation he had jumped off the Pyrmont Bridge in Sydney. His left foot was to become forever damaged. He was fortunate to have survived the jump. Years of tussles between the Australian bureaucracy and my parents did not resolve the lack of care for Frank. He would either be free to come and go as he liked, or, the alternative, he would be 'scheduled', and he would never come home. The idea of 'scheduling' Frank into an Australian institute filled us all with horror. There did not seem to be anything in between. The very term 'scheduled' brings Charles Dickens and Bedlam into focus. Even today, I would not want to hear Mental Health and Australia mentioned in the same sentence. At least, not during that period. When Frank jumped off the Pyrmont Bridge he had for some years joined that army of the dishevelled, the uncombed, and lost souls that roam streets, hovering between unreliable and vague sanity and death without much care by others except for the desperate parents or a rare kind person that would at times provide food, shelter and some encouraging words.

Two Dutch carers from Holland came to pick Frank up from Sydney and he was flown back to Holland with my parents. It would not have been easy to have a mentally ill person on a plane, but the Dutch Government would have complied with the relevant regulations. One can imagine! My parents were informed of what to expect for Frank in the care of Dutch social welfare and mental health. He had a room on his own with TV, and encouraged to play sport and swim. He would have his own income and be free to do with it what he liked (he bought his own clothes and cigarettes). My parents were at all times kept informed about his health, medication. He was given dental care, and his feet and eyes were looked after and maintained. His days would be spent with activities and work. At times, he would be taken in groups on outings, excursions, and holidays; even at one stage to France! My parents were free to visit, and Frank free to visit his parents, but always accompanied by nursing staff. Helvi and I remember once visiting Frank at his new place in Holland, and asked if we could speak to his doctor and staff. We were given a lunch, sat around the table talking to the psychiatrist, his doctor, and staff.

They were at pains to answer all our questions and concerns. An unbelievable and wonderful experience. A weight was lifted from our family. Why was that so difficult to achieve in Australia?

My parents also left Australia forever and decided to be with Frank and own extended family of brothers and sisters. A considerable number had moved into an age in tandem with themselves. Their numerous children were now adults with own families but back in Australia. Today, in 2015, the original children from my parents' migration are now retired as well, and care-free to enjoy life, paint the town red, or if not red, at least take a floating tour on the rivers of Europe, sipping champagne, view Habsburg's castles perched on steep cliffs, and rocky outposts. But going back to the seventies. My parents had put up their house for sale in Revesby that would afford them a little nest egg. It was for them the right thing to do. They would be with Frank and their own family. The rest of us had settled, married and had children of our own. And then, like a bolt of lightning, we decided, or rather I decided, to return to Australia... But of that...next time.

Return to Australia.

The decision to return to Australia came unexpectedly. I was the last one to recognize its coming. As noted before, things were steaming along nicely. Painting was in full flight. Money was being earned as a fully-fledged artist. I was teaching adults. Our children were growing and thriving. We lived in a lovely farm-house. The Shetlands were settled and the beady-eyed Barneveldt chickens were happy and laying generously. What more could one want? There are several possible explanations that led to this decision. None are valid enough on their own, but perhaps together, and in total, might shed some light on this sudden and strange 'out of the blue' return to Australia. Let me start on just a couple of explanations of events that I remember as if from yesterday.

We decided to go swimming in a small lake popular during those rare warm days that even rainy Holland sometimes gets rewarded with. The province that our village was situated in is the least populated area in Holland. At that time, one could still find small areas of wilderness to enjoy, without huge swarms of people crowding in on all pleasurable activities. When we arrived there were some people and kids about, but that only made it even more enjoyable. This little lake used to be a sand quarry but had been surrendered to Mum Nature when the sand digging had ceased. It was a lovely spot surrounded by bushes seeking shelter under pine trees. Included in those bushes was a haze of purple heather. There was laughter and joy about. The perfect day!

We all jumped in. It was a kind of jubilation, a celebration of unbridled joy and a fun day. There was a large family also jumping about, with a tribe of children skirmishing and splashing up and down in the shallow water, mucking about with a large log that they had dragged into the water. They seemed to talk in a foreign language. Perhaps they were Turkish or Moroccan immigrants. In any case, they had a lot of fun. The parents were looking on. All were safe. Out of the bushes all of a sudden a person of some grey authority appeared. He looked forbidding. Almost like something out of a faded book of doom or a lost page out The Treaty of Utrecht. He went to the edge of the water, and ordered in no uncertain manner for the children to take that unauthorized log of wood out of the water. The kids looked somewhat frightened. The parents got up to find out what the problem was that this killjoy figure seemed to have. An argument ensued after the parents wanted to find out the reason why this log seemed to be so difficult to accept in the water. At this stage, the man of authority could have just shrugged his shoulders and walked away. He did not. He started on a long explanation on what would happen if everyone took a log into the water. 'What then, he demanded. 'Suppose we all take a log? What then?' he added. A cloud came over the event. The kids dragged the log out of the water and back into the bushes. The parents said something in their own language and gave in, not wanting to risk a fine or Court appearance for non-compliance of an order. Order in Holland has to be maintained at all cost.

A similar event occurred a few months after the unauthorized log event. In the part of Holland that we lived in exists a lovely and unspoiled piece of original nature. It is called Mantingerzand. It was within a twenty minute drive. A very beautiful, original and unique nature reserve.

We decided to go for a picnic and had packed sandwiches to take with us for a lunch. Throughout this nature reserve are walking paths which one has to follow. Of course, in order to not disturb the uniqueness of this original piece of nature, it is pointed out and fully understandable, to stay within the pathways. As we were walking along, absorbing the beauty of the place, we all were getting hungry. The fresh air in nature does that, doesn't it? We decided to just stop, sit down on the pathway and eat our cheese and peanut sandwiches. Within a few minutes, and within the time-frame of having swallowed the first vigorous bites into our sandwich, the faded and dreaded figure of authority turned up on his bike. 'What do you think you are doing NOW?' he said. We turned pale and the kids looked frightened. 'We are eating sandwiches,' I stated with some hesitancy, in case we were doing something else or esoteric, considered to be so dreadful, it wasn't worth thinking about.

'Now just think a bit,' the grey man stated! We immediately started thinking feverishly but obediently. Our sandwiches were patiently waiting to be chewed further. But we had all gotten strangely un-hungry. 'Just imagine, just imagine.' The grey figure was now warming up to his favourite phrase (he had honed the wording in front of his proud wife the very night before). 'Just imagine if all of us would sit down and eat sandwiches in nature, just like that,' he said. 'What would happen then?' he asked. He looked at us (triumphantly) in turn.

We gave in, got up and resumed our walk. We put the patient sandwiches and thermos back in the bag and silently walked on.

So Much More to Law & Order and Compliance.

Of course, the idea of shifting home and hearth to a different continent because of a disallowance to eat peanut and cheese sandwiches while sitting down in a State protected nature-reserve is perhaps a bit too flighty to take seriously. It is just too silly for words. Holland is a small country and 'just imagine' if we all went around eating sandwiches willy nilly in nature reserves? Not a blade of grass would survive the onslaught of peanut butter and cheese sandwiches being flung about in the bushes by rebellious kids for whom nothing short of a Big Mac with Coke would suffice. Even if we did not sit down with the sandwiches, nature would not cope with the millions of feet trampling all over the place. The acidity of Coke vapours alone would kill the few remaining forests. Holland is wise to tell its citizens, you can look at the grass but stay off it!

No, there were other reasons for this sudden decision to leave when all seemed to go so well. It might well have to do with something that makes a country appreciated when living away from it. The very things that I disliked about our previous abode in Australia were the very things I now missed. I missed them sorely! It could well be the total contrast of the environment. Holland is neat, tidy and so well organised. Nothing out of place. Nothing allowed to be out of place.

Australia can be chaotic. It has the freedom to be so. Weeds are growing between the cracks on bitumen roads. Some footpaths would lift and stick up from battle hardened paper-bark tree roots, rampantly and disobediently growing upwards, without a diploma, permission or license. Sheets of rusted corrugation flapping merrily in the wind in a contemptuous dereliction. Car sales yards with yawning bonnets neck on neck and in between suburban houses. The rickety verandas enclosed with crinkle-glassed louvre windows. Some open like missing teeth, giving the inhabitant the opportunity to wind-dry unashamedly orange singlets with holes in it or to look at the belching diesel fumes of passing trucks.

After three years in Holland, our re-entry visas to Australia had run out. We had to go through the rigmarole of applying for migration. Our three children had Australian citizenship allowing a speedy permission to remigrate. Again, the buff coloured letter-heads came in handy. Australia was still in dire needs of painting. The 'good' kind of painting for houses and industry. The jovial consular official of the Australia embassy cracked a couple of jokes. We were almost back in Australia within those The Hague embassy walls. His top three or four shirt buttons were undone. He made us a coffee.

One of the more fortuitous events that we were totally unaware of while in Holland were the tumultuous political shenanigans that had occurred in Australia during our absence. There were scandals of unscrupulous money borrowings from shady Middle Eastern money merchants. There were love intrigues between married politicians. The world lapped it all up. Sensational exposure to scandal after scandal. Governments resigned, and the Australian dollar collapsed. After flying back and landing in Sydney, my brother picked us up from the airport. We were to live in their house while he and his three children were going to travel to Europe. In exchange, we gave them our trusted VW Kombi parked at our parents' place in Holland.

As we again scoured around to find a place to live, there was no question we would again find our feet back in old trusted Balmain. Our kids were enrolled in the school that our eldest daughter had been going to before we went to Holland in search of the artist salary. The very house that we used to admire before our departure to

Holland was for sale. Can you believe it? A five bedroom house made of sandstone with a large garden. We were told Germaine Greer had lived in it during her wild bra-less student days. We were totally but very pleasantly knocked off our socks when we converted our Dutch guilders into Australian dollars. The devaluation meant we came back with more than what we had left with. Much more. How could Australia be any friendlier? We bought the house with a small mortgage.

It had turned out so well. Again!

This Matter of Right Choices.

In summing up, the choice to return to Australia from Holland was made spontaneously. Helvi was happy to stay but also happy to return. She has much less trouble with the perceived pros and cons of this country or that country. To just get on is much more in her domain than mine. I mull and procrastinate, and still make rash decisions. Logical decisions are an oxymoron.

The reasons given can be seen as both wise and unwise. Both countries have good and not so good qualities depending on personal likes or dislikes. To shine further light on what happened back in 1976 seems an exercise that might be futile, and runs the risk of boring the reader who could already be somewhat stretched in accepting this chain of indecisive events.

I do remember missing the good times with my extended family of brothers and sister with their spouses, and their children in Australia. Another item not to be ignored was the lure of the bush. It is rather comforting to know you can just walk into the Australian bush for days, never need to meet another soul. This makes for great therapy, but also great murder scenarios. Skeletons are sometimes discovered of people gone missing years before. Australia is even big enough for that! Some call it Lebensraum.

The sea of life is what we make of it, and mulling over past events is what this exercise is all about. I write down what happened in the past, hopefully without invoking even more guilt or judgement. This is a luxury that I give to the readers. There is no greater naval gazing than writing memoirs. The dressing up of calling it an Autobiography seems a bit haughty if not pretentious. It is not as if this writer is an Obama or the latest Pope! Even so, it is the best I can come up with in doing something useful. Apart from all that, it keeps me off the streets.

If I remember right, we arrived back in Australia in the beginning of June 1976 and moved into our house around the beginning of August, coinciding with arrival of all our belongings. Those belongings were packed in Holland in two large wooden crates measuring together a bit over seventeen cubic metres. I received a letter from Customs that the goods had arrived, and that, after inspection by custom officers, I could arrange to get them picked up, and delivered to our house in Balmain. The Custom letter also gave the sage advice to take a jemmy-bar to prise open the lids of the wooden crates.

After arrival at the depot it took about half-a-day to find the crates amongst thousands of other crates. It had Oosterman written on it and that was of some comfort. However, opening the lids proved to be difficult. Even to get on top of the crates was going to be very difficult (sorry, 'challenging'). It was years later when the word 'difficult' would be banned, and changed into 'challenge.' The psychologists have a lot to answer for by changing words around that make us believe life is easier. Later on, the word 'challenge' was primed up even further and has now morphed into 'solutions'. We all know that after paying to get ourselves psycho-analysed we end up accepting there is nothing to life's problems that can't be overcome by using and finding 'solutions'. I wrote before about our local butcher selling 'meat solutions'. Huge trucks and road trains thunder along our highways with 'logistics' written on their tarpaulins, bringing 'solutions' all around our country.

A friendly truck-driver gave me a leg-up onto the top of the crate. How to open the lids allowing for Custom Officer's inspection when standing on top of it? The logistics were challenging. The Custom Officer arrived, and with help of the friendly truck driver managed to open the lids. He poked around a bit. He wasn't all that enthusiastic in looking for wood-worm or other possible infestations of bugs that Australia was very weary off. Most people that have flown into Australia might remember the Customs carnival going through the plane cross armed, holding two spray cans above their heads and spraying the perplexed passengers still sweetly restrained, sitting in their seats! All in an effort to safeguard Australia from nasty foreign-born flies and insects. Of course, no country in the world suffers more from flies than Australia!

This Life of Camping Out.

The moving about, even just in the mind, can be unsettling. Ten days in Bali, ok, let's live there. Two days at the Eco-village in Queensland, let's go! No wonder my Helvi is getting nervous. 'You will still take your own with you. The black curmudgeon sits on your shoulder night and day,' she says. 'People know that but they can't see it,' is added for extra impact. The dream of living in likewise communities is what plagued me since birth. And that's how it goes. The attraction of living somewhere where low impact on nature is shared within a community does pull. That's apart from the bonus of a ban on fences, especially colour-bond fences, and electricity burning air conditioning.

It is true that the social skills of easy laughter and merrymaking in company of others is wanting. A demeanour of a seriously looking man exudes and leaps in front like a warning on the fly-spray well before actually meeting. It can't be helped, even when wearing my partial dentures. However, lately I do go around smiling more which helps, but only in combination when walking with our Jack Russell, 'Milo'. I got a smile last Tuesday at Aldi's while tying up Milo at the trolley bay. I saw the woman again inside the shop as she was bending over the carrots next to the capsicums. My H is the opposite. She has a Mona Lisa smile. It comes naturally. She feels the smile. People often talk to her, which I envy. She draws in people. I seem to repel, but am working on it. It is never too late, and I can still climb stairs two steps at a time. That has to be worth something.

With the autobiography -or memoirs, if you prefer- it seems to have stalled. The moving about has rippled into the consciousness of everyday living. The living in a town-house of seven others in the compound is magnifying the stark differences between communal design and the exclusive or excluding design where privacy dominates. People might peer from behind the blinds. Perhaps not even that! A garage door rolls up, but the owner is already in the car. We can't see him as he drives off.

In Eco-village last week we saw people moving about inside their houses. There was proof of life. Some were working in the garden. Children were running wild but in total safety. Kangaroos were lulling about, sunning themselves on grass with the black water-hens picking morsels out of the compost bins. A man with binoculars was trying to spot birds. He had lost his wife some time back but he had not given up. He recorded all birds and had brought cameras to photograph whatever he felt like photographing. He was happy.

You know that, at the age of over seventy five, the egg-timer is slowly running out of sand. One is not totally without optimism. My Mum was ninety six when she died. A good omen. Dad was seventy eight and smoked, but enjoyed it till the end. At his funeral, and going back afterwards, my Mum cleaned for the last time his ashtray. He was still alive the day before and drove his car. He hated hospitals and going to the doctor. No sooner after he was taken to a hospital, he died. So all up, if we split the difference (one has to be fair), it would allow another ten years before the egg-timer would run out my sand.

I would be happy with that. So much still to smile about.

The Forbidden Words Formed Long Queues.

The seventies were already getting very modern. You would have thought the world belonged to those wearing jeans and perms. Yes, that's right, I too had a perm done. It was a sign of male emancipation. The journey (and who is not on a journey now-a-days?) of freeing the shackles of the sixties started in my case a few years earlier with a vasectomy performed by two female doctors, one was Dr Simcock. A good omen. I remember both of them crouched down at the bottom of the bed, intent on the snapping of my vas deference. The perm ensured acceptance and added to confidence. The vasectomy a discontinuation of the family who already counted three in an over-populated world. Why could the world of blond curls and untidy beards not be an outward sign for those who owned the world?

What was not so modern though, and it seems ludicrous today, was that words were still banned. Portnoy's Complaint and Lolita were banned. The literary experts whose job it was to look after our morals, and were employed as Censors, needed an ambulance after they had ploughed through those books. They were maimed for life. That's what words can do. Words like cunt and masturbation, breasts and erection, and the unspeakable cock or penis. When the books were finally released, pent up by the tens of thousands on our wharfs in grey camouflaged wooden crates, pandemonium broke out. Police on horseback had to whip back and restrain rain-coat wearing men. Blunt-Stone boot wearing women, all queuing up to get a copy and read all about banned words. There were no signs, as feared, of anyone going in a sexual frenzy. There were no rapports of fornication on the foot-path outside Hans's delicatessen with the signs of Heisse KnackWurst for sale, or indeed inside the KFC take-away.

A few years earlier, similar horse-backed police had to restrain theatre patrons in front of the Metro in Kings Cross where after weeks of parliamentary arguments, the musical Hair was finally allowed to be shown. Permission was given after agreements were reached whereby during the 'nude' part all the actors and dancers were strictly to adhere no body part would swing or move about. A large army canvas would be hoisted up by a crane. The nudeness had to be done in absolute stillness. A single quiver in testicles or breasts and the show would be cancelled. It was an electrifying moment for Australia. Slowly, the large canvas was lifted. The audience mouse-still. Not a flitting of an eyelash. Real nudes. Unbelievable. Afterwards, the patrons silently left the theatre, overwhelmed by it all. Many went home, got undressed, and looked in the mirror! Next morning people queued up for the bus. Life seemed to go on the same as before. It always does. On weekends, the lawnmowers happily rattled on and the suburban nature strip wasn't forgotten either. Petunias were being planted, rockeries cemented and fences re-painted.

It was always thus.

Auto-Biography to Memoirs.

Now that the medical investigations of physical health and other possible upcoming frailties in the future have been dealt with I can perhaps go back to my earlier musings about the past. They were originally all bundled under the somewhat pretentious title of Auto-biography. Towards the end it morphed into autobiography, or as now referred to as memoirs. Perhaps memoirs is the most suitable. Who knows? It has a hint of someone getting ready for the softness of blissful forgetfulness, but would still like to leave behind a story of when that was not so. A kind of evidence based on the purpose that life once might have held. Not that life is totally without purpose now. The garbage bin has to be put out, not forgetting the alternative weeks (fortnightly pension day) that the yellow lidded recycle bin has to be put outside but the red bin always weekly. A routine that is now well established. I never forget. There is something very endearing about those bits of routine. It beds us down, makes us feel secure. One can imagine the millions of refugees on the run from bombs and terror. All routine of daily life stolen at a moment's notice. You can see it in their eyes. Frightened of what the future holds. How fortunate we are. It is only the luck of our birth that separates us from those running the gauntlet of many borders, clambering over train windows, desperate to escape from the uncertainty. Nothing more than that.

As I remembered, after our family's return from Holland in 1976 we moved into our house back in Sydney's Balmain, and had taken delivery of our furniture, and all other remnants of our previous three years in Holland. I enjoyed the artist's salary, had some exhibitions, sold some paintings, but also missed our large extended family. The Australian bush, as well as the disorder of rusted roofs and the chaos of Parramatta Rd, beckoned. Those yawning second-hand car sales yard seemed so attractive. A funny thing. The Dutch sense of order and discipline had taken its toll. The breathing space that we have in Australia is not to be underestimated. When life got back to normal, the children back to school and a smooth transition into work and paying bills, life resumed its path with routine getting established once more. The garage was transformed into a place to make the stretchers for paintings. Part of it was made into a darkroom. I suddenly developed a keenness for taking photographs, and with my brother used to develop our own black and white shots of people and city/landscapes. A very prolific period of paintings followed. I entered again many paintings in local art competitions which many councils annually held all over Australia. Balmain was attractive to artists, and in our street alone there was a group of them all beavering away inside their studios. Some of the artists were very 'arty' and used to delve into mysticism, or were very esoteric to the extreme. Bach remedy was used for everything, even giving birth or a dog's broken leg. Dreadlocks and smoking dope was very popular, and so were music of a kind sung by the massively curled Carly Simon, especially 'You're So Vain'. Of course, we were united against war, especially nuclear war, and used to march in rallies together with Patrick White, whose popularity as a Noble Price winning writer of fame seems now to have waned.

The Country of the Long Weekend.

The long weekend would inevitably start by packing the van and going camping. We have most of our photo albums packed with camping shots. It became another art form. In the days when our children were young, camping was big. Especially down and up from Sydney. The bush was still bush, and it wasn't till caravan parks started to appear that camping was pushed in the background. Now, camping grounds are controlled, and camper vans and caravans are parked neck on neck. It is like going to the local Drive-In of yesteryears. Watch Quo Vadis with a two kilo pack of pop-corn. The kids and

Mum dressed in pyjamas, ready to hit the sack after driving home. This weekend we had the grandsons staying with us after Mum had them all week. School holidays used to be the worst time for Mums, the stuff of nightmares. Now, of course, with the average family of 1.9 children, it should be a much easier ride for Mums. But is it? Sipping a coffee with our grandkids yesterday, I noticed the grim-faced Mums walking the Bowral streets with kids in tow. There was an air of resignation, but also of a hope springing eternally. Another couple of days and all will be back at school. Order again, and bored kids getting what they deserve, an education.

In the fifties and sixties, camping shops were big business and tents used to be put up on show. Parramatta Road had huge camping shops and one would go there as an outing, feel inspired by stakes, axes, pocket knives, foldable water containers and mouth-watering port-a-loos. Tents were made above those shops by Hungarian experts or strongly calved ex Austrian mountaineers. We loved camping and used to hack away the Lantana to clear a spot for our tents. With bush-saws we would cut a dead tree and sit around the camp-fire drinking cheap hot wine spiced with cloves. The headaches next morning were legendary and have till now never been surpassed. All this has changed. On the highways, enormous double bogey vans are being pulled along by equally enormous multi-storied vans. There are air-condition units on top and at the back of the van. At times, a smaller car is being towed along and multi layers of canoes with mountain-bikes strapped on top. I am not sure, but I suspect that multi-electronic devices are being held by those that are not driving. The selfie sticks at the ready even while driving, images and selfies are instantly being beamed around the world by the kids sitting on the lower deck of the SUV. Our camping days are over and I could not imagine crawling out of a tent with a bad headache and then having to cook porridge on a dead fire. This weekend no camping, instead I got up early and prepared the pancake mixture with the butter milk bought the previous day. It is the least I could do and the kids love it more than camping. Things have changed. After a few days with us, and before the Mum came to pick them up, I had promised them a bit of a gourmet supper. Apart from pancakes, the kids have also been encouraged into liking sea-food. If there is one thing I want achieved, it is for them to enjoy the delights of herrings and mussels. Even during the grimmest of times, a good herring or bowl of steaming mussels would pull me through during the blight of my suburban youth! It does no harm to kids and is as good as camping. I bought two kilos of mussels, and after steaming them up in some white wine, crushed tomatoes and lots of garlic, were consumed by a fervour not even experienced during their much earlier discovery of the iPhone. It was a great weekend. One of the best, really.

The Camper Van. Are We There Yet?

When still in Holland, we drove around in a VW Campervan. Strictly speaking, it was not, but we made it a van that could be slept in. With some help from self-tapping screws, eyelets and wires, we fashioned curtains. We took the back seat out, and with chipboard made a bed base of some three quarter queen size width, enough for both of us if sleeping in spoon fashion (or forks when amorous). We used the space underneath this bed for storage. After our return to Australia, I promptly bought another VW van with three rows of seats. What I forgot to check was the size of the engine. The one in Holland had a two litre engine, while the one in Australia was a 1600cc engine. A big difference, especially fully laden and towing a small trailer. The road that had to be turned left to go to our favourite camping spot was still a dirt road and muddy after rain. During wet days it would almost take an hour to travel the 20km or so. There were some hills that were steep, and it would not be difficult to find oneself almost unable to either go down or up those hills.

The advertisement that had the young kids asking, 'Are we there yet, Daddy?' must have been inspired by so many families travelling with children. The on-board DVD had yet to be discovered. Even that gadget has now been overtaken by iPhones, pad and pods, and heaven knows what else kids are now stooped over, pushing buttons with a rapid-fire machine-gun speed. Has anyone noticed how nimble the kids are with the gadget being manoeuvred with their two thumbs writing commands on that little keyboard? Truly amazing. When I put my finger down, the whole keyboard follows, or the English changes into Chinese. We still try and engage our grandkids with the game of 'I spy, I spy, with my little eye', and as yet, and most times, even the fifteen year old still responds during the trip to Sydney and back. Squabbling between young siblings inside a moving car is the stuff of family punch-ups at the rest stop, which can never come quick enough. Dear H is an angel during car trips and the punch-ups are usually prevented. If it persists, we threaten a sound belting or an ejection from the car on an isolated bush-track. ;) The usual squabble with grandkids is the same as it was with our own kids forty or more years ago, with… "Mum…Mum, he has taken over my space, and has his hands near me." H said, "Move back and try and stay there, you are annoying your sister." After five minutes of peace. "Mum…Mum, she is laughing at me now, again." The 'again' doubles the annoyance. H said, "Stop laughing at your sister, we are nearly there." Again, almost immediately (and I am white knuckled over the steering wheel) "Mum…Mum… She is yucky looking again and has her foot on my foot." H takes out the expendable steering lock and swings it threateningly towards the back seat. It stays quiet for a whole twelve minutes. It starts again. "Mum…Mum…Dad…Dad… are we there yet?" Of course, the real cruelty is for kids to be locked up in a small confined space. Every time watching young kids, they hop and skip, move about constantly. They can't even take one single straight step without doing gymnastics or somersaulting on the footpath. They are growing up and a car is not for kids. Even so, at least there are electronic gadgets that help.

Are we there yet?

The Caravan and Uncle Bill with Dusty Lungs.

When school holidays were coming, the list would be ticked off. Sleeping bags, tents, tarpaulins for over the tents, rubber sheets for under the tents, water containers, fishing rods, papoose, saucepans, cutlery, plates, cups, beakers, books, toys, barbeque tongs, matches, wine casks, food. Bewildering arrangement of breakfast cereals, potatoes, tinned sardines, tuna, some biscuits, crackers, cheeses, Bismarck herrings, sausages, some lollies (for during the car trip), Hanso-plast plasters, a solid supply of headache tablets, unguents for driver's constipation, food poisoning and/or for frequent and copious discharge of abnormal pains tablets. Fly sprays, mosquito coils, sun tan oils, pink sun tan burn medication, mosquito screens for tent openings. Matches, swimming gear including boards and body surfing equipment. Spare fishing hooks, lines and weights. A fish scaling knife, fish filleting knife, a fish net, lemons for the oysters. Children and shorts, lots of clothing and spare shoes. Children's friends, including James Crow and others. Finally, the esky to keep the milk in! It was all put together with military order and discipline the day before. Each item would be ticked off carefully. After a few years we got a trailer to put it all in. This required another tarpaulin to put over it, in case the polystyrene surf boards would fly out. This then required a strong rope like netting to put over the tarpaulin to stop it from flapping. The car had to be fitted with a tow-bar. I often had severely bruised shins having walked around the van checking things, and walking straight into the tow-bar. I would limp for the entire holiday.

When the children reached teen years we went over to the caravan owners' side. No more tents! We were so over all the rigmarole of packing and unpacking stuff. Many times we would have downpours and packed up everything sodden. This then had to be spread out over the garden lawn back home in Balmain. The drying and storing took days, and whatever rest and recreation we enjoyed during camping was soon soaked up in all this work. Our faces had become lined and crinkly. Camping became a chore after so many years. We needed rest from all that. We bought the caravan. It had a baffling name: As is, is! It was onsite at a terrific spot overlooking the ocean. "Dad, Dad shall we buy it?" Before this new period, we always looked a bit down on caravan owners. Somehow, they were not real campers, and not really people worthy of sitting around with at camp-fires. They even used to have antennas on the roofs of the vans and could be heard watching the Dick van Dyke show or worse, the hideous loud cackle of I Love Lucy infiltrating the lantana and waking the possums. I don't really know how we made the transition from tent to caravan. Was it a mixture of hypocrisy and swallowing pride? Perhaps it was, because we got to know a couple of ex coal-miners suffering from dusty lungs. They lived permanently in caravans with large canvas annexes. A kind of happy mixture of tents and caravans.

One of them we got to know as Uncle Pudding. He was rather shy, but very good with our kids. They loved him. He would go fishing with a mate who had a boat and give us part of his catch afterwards. Despite the condition of his lungs, he smoked ready-rubs. I can still see him taking a pluck of tobacco out of its metal container, rub it in his hands while keeping the Tally-Ho tobacco paper sheet between his lips. He would roll his ciggy, lick the edge of his Tally-Ho and light up. He kept his camp site scrupulously clean. The happy sound of his raking in the morning could be heard each day. For many years he was a figure known to us and many campers. But suddenly Uncle Bill was gone. He had finally succumbed to dusty lungs.

The Safari Suit.

We are now going back to a period when our children numbered just two.

It was a long time ago! We were living in our second house on Sydney's Harbour peninsula, Balmain. As you might remember, we lived in a one bedroom apartment in a somewhat bohemian area called Pott's Point, which is next to -or part of- Kings Cross, Sydney. It was an area of artists, crooks, prostitutes, sandaled souteneurs, and priests. There were also many delicatessen where one could buy real coffee, prosciutto, cheeses not named 'tasty', and books. If I remember correctly, there was also special dispensation given to some Euro-continental shops allowing to stay open after 6pm. It was still frowned upon as decadent by some who tried desperately to uphold decent 'peace and quiet' Anglo closed up traditions. This all during the sixties when our marriage was still young, sprightly and sprouting first babies.

The one bedroom apartment was soon crowded with birth of our second daughter. We bought a very old and rickety weather board cottage that just had one large sitting-kitchen-dining-bathroom downstairs and two small bedrooms upstairs. The downstairs would originally have had rooms but the previous architect owner had taken all walls out leaving just one spacious room that looked out over a glorious and vibrant harbour. In those day it was always sunny. That the bathroom was part of our sitting area could not have worried the architect, nor did it us. In the middle of this room was a round wood burning cast-iron heater with the name 'Broadway' on it. It was lined with stone on the inside, and as a chimney had a large galvanized pipe going through the ceiling and upstairs bedrooms, ending finally through both levels on top of the roof. It was capped by a Chinaman's hat to keep out rain. It heated the whole house during winter with cut up old wooden railway sleepers. The cottage had a waxed wooden floor downstairs and upstairs I painted the floors white. This was a typical workman's cottage that might have years back housed a family with three or four children with a husband who could well have been employed in the stevedoring industry. He might have smelled of tar, salt and rope each time he arrived home with his wife frying mutton chops for dinner while their children played outside.

The harbour in front of this cottage was less than a hundred meters away, and always busy with tug-boats towing large boats. The house would vibrate each time the propellers reversed. We had hammered or knocked together our own furniture and made do with little. Milk came in glass bottles and bread delivered by the baker. This would be announced by barking dogs. Even roosters were still around. We could afford the luxury of a nappy service and had a second hand washing machine, of which the only drawback was that the pump had packed up. No worries, we sucked on the hose to get the gravity of flow going, and let it run into our court yard. That is how it was. Not anymore. At Christmas we had parties and fondues with friends and family sitting on planks suspended between paint drums while listening to the Beatles' Sargent Pepper, or Peter, Paul & Mary thumping out from homemade giant speaker boxes with twelve inch woofers, tweeters and cross-overs. Did we not also drink cheap headache wine squeezed out of bladders into nice fluted glasses? We would meet and compare the tie-dyes. Wives sometimes dressed in pantsuits, men with hair the longer the better, jeans dangerously flared. The enormous shoulder pads were yet to come, waiting in the wings. They were the best years. But aren't all years of past the best?

During that time when things had settled, and with money coming in, Helvi decided to visit her family in Finland, taking our two young children. Our youngest daughter would be carried in a papoose while her sister was old enough to walk at airports during change-overs and helpful in carrying her own little bag. It was quite a trip from Sydney with another plane to catch in Finland to the closest airport where her family lived. Finland is a huge country, larger even than the UK. It was going to be a six week holiday and I would be on my own. I could hardly wait for their return but had to do with receiving letters for the time being and the rare phone call. It was a lonely time and I missed my family.

I made a choice than that still haunts me today. It is forever raked up and retold to friends ready for a good laugh. I bought a wine-red knitted Safari suit. It had flared pants and a double breasted jacket held together with brass gold buttons and a belt of the same material. The jacket's belt was held well above my waste. It was the height of fashion. The trouser belt was the same, and also with a gold buckle. The whole outfit was ostentatiously knitted and screamed out for attention. I also bought something resembling shoes that were made in Egypt. The toe part of those shoes was made of rope that was coiled around the toe and heel part above the sole, while in between was a cream leather-like material with a buckle on top. I completed the whole outfit with a modest gold chain worn unobtrusively but magnificently opulent, around my neck. My idea was to look a new man, or at least a reborn man. A proud prince of unsurpassed passion and vibrant vitality. I wanted to impress my Helvi. I looked, of course, a one hit pop star failure, but at the time wasn't aware of this, blinded as usual by foolish folly.

On the right, Susanna and Natasha in Finland

I went to the airport on the day of my family's return to Sydney. All good things come to an end. As my little family passed through customs and into the arrival hall I spotted them first. The look on my wife's face was utter disbelief soon followed by scowling disapproval. 'What are you wearing now?' she said. My daughters too looked frightened. Of course, we drove home all excited to be together again, but Helvi kept looking at my suit and shaking her head. I never wore the suit again, nor ever shopped for clothes without Helvi having an input. I am fashion blind. The shoes went into the slow combustion Broadway.

The Russian Trip.

I'll try and find my box of photos that I took while I was in the USSR during the mid-eighties. I don't write in diaries so my dates have to be given much leeway by those readers diligent and tenacious enough to keep following my words. Most of what I seem to write is from many decades ago. With old age also comes a kind of carelessness. Why not enjoy at least that luxury? What is true so far is that back in the eighties, or so, I noticed an advertisement in the travel section of our biggest newspaper, the Sydney Morning Herald, about an all-inclusive trip to the USSR.

Moscow University

It included, as one would expect, Moscow and St Petersburg, and would end in London. All hotels and meals were included. Russia was also going through a profound change whereby its last leader was being challenged by a more modern and forward looking man named Mikhail Gorbachev. He was the last of the Soviet Union's Presidents. I have now found the box of photos taken by the Russian Camera. It had a very powerful shutter mechanism which reminded me somewhat of my BSA 22 single shot rifle that I used for rabbit hunting during the late fifties. The shutter spring must have been so strong the film was exposed twice during the release of the shutter on the bounce back.

A group drinking. I did not investigate what it was they were drinking. It might have been some soft drink or Vodka. Who knows?

Lomonosov Moscow State University is so big, students have been found at an advanced age simply because they lost their way to the exit, and finally gave up, preferring instead to live in its library with 9,000,000 books, 2,000,000 in foreign languages. The university has 1 ,000,000 square meters floor area in 1000 buildings and structures, with its 8 dormitories housing over 12,000 students of its 40,000 students and 300 km of utility lines. All free, of course, even to foreign students.

The Russians are big on visiting graves and so they should. Some say you can tell a culture by the way they look after their departed souls. The graves are often surrounded by pink and white Syringa vulgaris (lilac), are well kept, and thankfully not a plastic flower in sight. As you dear readers might know, I too am fond of graves and grave yards. There is something so life confirming about them, especially when you know it befalls everybody. A life well lived deserves a nice farewell and a good grave. There were some Australian girls in our group who thought they would like to shop. It has often puzzled me, travelling and shopping. They hadn't done their homework on the USSR. I found it to be a very fascinating insight and absolutely enjoyed my stay there. People were curious and knew a lot about literature and art. I was ashamed to admit some students knew more about Australian writers than I did. On the Moscow-St Petersburg train I met a German speaking Russian woman named Lily who kept giving me sugar cubes dipped in Absinthe, and when I told her I was an artist she told the rest of our train compartment. I was just about carried on the shoulders of the Russian travellers. But of that more next time.

Moscow and Overnight Train to St Petersburg. Valley of Lilly.

(About 1985) After a week or so in Moscow, with the obligatory viewing of Red Square, the mile long queue at the Lenin Mausoleum, the Stalin built but magnificent underground railway with marbled statues and chandeliers, we all looked forward to an evening at the theatre featuring, An American in Paris, by American composer of Russian parentage, George Gershwin. Next day, we all took a late evening overnight train to St Petersburg. It was in July, very hot, and the days were interspersed with short but violent lightning storms. I was surprised that the giant down pipes of those large roofed buildings jettisoned the pelting rain straight onto the footpath, whereby pedestrians had to perform large leaps into the air to not get washed into the kerbs. I was astonished how high the Russians could leap, but it gave me a better perspective on the Bolshoi Ballet phenomenon.

The Hermitage. St-Petersburg

The overnight trip to St Petersburg has been covered earlier but is now buried at the bottom of this pile, and in any case, my memory might well have shifted to even greater heights. Here another retell. After getting on-board we were given the seats as shown on the pre-booked tickets. My compartment had a married couple and a woman of typical generous Russian proportion and spirit. The two compartments behind me were taken up by an American group of singers who had performed in Moscow and were now on their way to St Petersburg as well. We soon settled, and when I took a walk around my wagon I noticed the Americans who, after introduction, told me they were part of a choir. As I told them I was Australian they were keen for me to give an impromptu performance of a Paul Hogan 'Crocodile Dundee' and several versions of, 'Goodyaj, howszego'en maitey?' I obliged but quickly escaped back to my cabin. I can only perform on my own without an audience or mirror. The woman and couple introduced themselves and so did I. The Russian woman's name was Lily and she could speak some German. One has to understand we were all going to sleep together so a kind of bonhomie and familiarity might ensure a reasonable and peaceful slumber later on. Russian trains do not segregate, but at least in USSR sleeper trains sleeping is not fraught with fear of an opportunistic sex maniac creeping in. That seems to be more the domain of those cultures that believe men and women are so entirely different they ought to be separated from birth whenever possible. For some, to attack remains the only option to get together.

Lily became instantly the epitome of what their race is known for. A socially inclusive and talkative person. Friendly and keen to exchange talk on almost anything and everything. It was easy for me when we could also talk in German, but I am sure that even without a common language she would have seen that as a minor obstacle, easily overcome by gesture and body language, facial expressions. It was a hot and somewhat brooding thunderstorm threatening train journey. We were all sweating profusely, and while talking, Lily would pat and dab her generously forthcoming bosom with a crocheted hanky (I remember it well). She kept sprinkling with Eau de Cologne number 4711. We exchanged small talk the best we could, of which I have forgotten most but not all. What I did not forget is what ensued after she asked me what I did. 'Ich bin ein Kunstler Und Lehrer,' I answered ('I am an artist and teacher'). Well, it was instant pandemonium. You would know that teachers in Eastern Europe, and especially Finland and former USSR countries, are regarded and revered like lawyers and doctors, if not a new Dostoevsky or a burgeoning Tolstoy. To be an artist and teacher is like being two doctors in one.

She took out a small bottle of a greenish colour, and poured some of the liquid in a metal beaker. The cabin immediately smelt strongly of aniseed. She also had a packet of sugar cubes which she had opened earlier, and given me some. She went around the wagon telling all that here was an Australian artist on board, while sharing the aniseed dipped sugar cubes all round. They all came, and wanted to inspect this Australian teacher – artist. It was my moment of fame. When things calmed down we retired back to our cabin while she kept up talk while dabbing bosom and giving absinthe laced sugar. Around midnight we had enough, and as the aniseed euphoria and drowsiness was starting to wear off, all decided to go to sleep. The couple and Lily promptly pulled the beds off the wall. We all took turns going to the corridor, allowing ablutions and getting ready for bed. I took the top bunk and Lily the bottom one. We were woken up early by the train lady conductor and given tea and sweet bread which famously gets served in large, very ornate silver teapots with drinking glasses held in equally ornate silver holders with swan-necked ears.

We had arrived at St Petersburg.

I Hope Your Culture is normal.

I thought I knew culture, or at least the average normal person's understanding of its meaning. But nothing surprised me more than when I got acquainted with a different, totally new form of culture, never experienced before. I also know that many people take rests on chairs, chaise lounges, settees, fauteuils, or even the simple piano stool. There is nothing odd about man's need for the occasional rest, even on a stool. But... I am getting ahead of myself; this tale of surprise and discovery of a new kind of culture needs time to ripen and mature. Ecoutez sil vous plait, and get a little closer to the book.

Over the last week or so I have been busy with domestic things. Paying bills, emptying the dishwasher, putting bins on the street, and even doing a thorough vacuum with the hand held one instead of the robovac. As readers might remember, some weeks ago I gave in, relented, bought an automatic vacuum cleaner that roams the rooms and ferrets around corners and underneath book shelves in between beds and saucepans. I find it fascinating to watch, seeing how it sends signals out to avoid obstacles and dead corners. The Robovac does a fair job, but with rough coated Jack Russell Milo, one needs to do a hand-held in between. On top of that I had to prepare myself for working this Saturday handing out 'How to Vote' cards for the Green party, of which I have been a member for just a few months. The state of NSW is having an election with everyone at fever pitch. The dogs are howling and swallows are flying erratically. They know it, too. I also fitted in a quick visit to the Moss Vale Medical Centre to check on a persistent pesky stomach bug. The good doctor from Indian background, whom I had not met before, did a good job, asking me all the relevant questions. History, if any, of stomach problems, family background, dodgy genes, fainting spells, giddiness, what job I did, smoke, drink etc.? He finally prodded around my stomach, but nothing painful or abnormal, and suggested I do some kind of what I understood a culture test. I agreed and thought any culture in Australia will do me, even if it is just the usual blood test. He wrote out the pathology note and as the pathologist outfit is next to the medical centre he suggested I do it straight away. The sooner the better, he smiled and shook my hand.

Helvi and I always go together to doctors as we do to shops or just walking around with Milo. In fact, we are probably noticed on our walks as a couple who are inseparable. Helvi glanced over to the lady behind the pathology counter and smiled. I too smiled and handed over the pathology request form. She read the doctor's note and smiled encouragingly. 'Have you done a stool culture before?' she asked. The penny dropped. I knew this culture were no ordinary culture, let alone a B's ninth symphony or viewing of the pyramids of Cheops. Of all of life's foibles, how did it come to this? I used to play in a sandpit and dreamt of castles.

'No, I haven't done that before,' I answered. 'I'll get you the necessary kit,' said the still smiling nurse. I wasn't smiling. The horror of what was now to come became clear. I looked back and Helvi was smiling broadly. For some reason women seem to find this a really amusing procedure for men to undergo. The nurse said: 'There are just two small containers you need to fill with a small scoop fitted on the back of each lid. You fill the small ones from the big container,' she added. I sunk below vision, and meekly said something like, 'Far-out,' or 'Can't wait'. The nurse's eyes met mine and a moment of some embarrassment was acknowledged, and with a smile she winked. It helped. She had seen all this before and she understood. By now, the nurse was really being encouraged by Helvi, having to keep her mouth covered to hide her mirth and smile, and yet the nurse had the nous to further explain, 'The large bowl is for putting it in the toilet bowl to catch your stool.' This last remark should have reached its zenith of relevant stool culture information. It did not. More was yet to come. 'You can use the scoop on the back of the smaller container's lid to fill each of them,' she said. 'You must also give details of date and time of each stool 'production' on the label, and number them as a one or a two.

Don't forget to wash the big container or use a new one each time. An ice-cream container will do,' she added. By this time the nurse was openly smiling and I was beyond caring. It would have been far worse if it had all been done in all seriousness. I mean, how could this possibly be a serious issue?

Even so, I hope that the future doesn't hold anymore medical cultural events like this one. I would much prefer to see Wagner's ring cycle.

P.S. I played along, wanting to be seen as suffering the ultimate crestfallen male with his fragile ego, hitting the very lows of the absurdity in his idea of masculinity. The very idea of a real man scooping his own faeces is unlimited material for comedy and laughter. It was very funny, and a bit of a show for the other patients sitting in chairs waiting their turn while listening in.

Life gets complicated but you have to face up to it, even when it includes strange cultures.

My Box Camera.

A few weeks ago I bought a book by Gunther Grass (umlaut) titled, 'The Box'. Its cover features a box camera and the words 'Tales from the Darkroom.' It is funny how a picture is able to recall memories deeply buried in the ashes of time passed all too soon. It was during my last year at high school in The Hague when rumours of my parents wanting to migrate to Australia were vaguely doing the rounds. I was fifteen. I happened to pass a camera shop and became instantly smitten by cameras that were displayed in the shop window. My Dad was a camera fan, and had one of those cameras that one could focus on the subject by a lens that was able to be moved backwards and forwards by a concertina type action. I think it was a Leica camera. However, with his six children running around the dining table (while shouting), and the Dutch rainy weather forever keeping us inside, his photography took a background stance. I don't think he took many photos that I can remember, except some years later after migration that he sent back to his parents (my paternal grandparents) whom he never saw again. My Mum lost her parents at ten years of age during the Spanish flu epidemic. When the migration plans became certain, I was taken out of school, and within days was working delivering fruit and vegetables to different embassies which The Hague was full of. I did those deliveries on a sturdy steel bike with huge handle bars and a large cane basket fitted over the front wheel. It was an industrial bike build specific for deliveries. The season was heading towards winter and storms were normal. However, I had my mind set on this box camera that I looked at numerous time in the window of the camera shop. Perhaps I inherited my Dad's obsession gene. I just had to have that camera.

My greatest joy was when a delivery had to be made to the American Embassy. I was friendly with the kitchen staff, and practiced my English I had been taught with two years at primary, and four years at high school. I would be given a hot soup with a tip that made my heart leap into my throat. I had started to smoke already, and apart from the generous tips was also given packets of Camel. Can you believe and understand my total happiness? Smoking in the fifties was regarded as a form of maturity, and for men at least, almost a healthy habit to engage in. Even doctors gave it the nod of approval while wearing the stethoscope with white jacket.

I did also at times try and get my hand underneath the wrapped up fruit, and remember snitching a few grapes, while I single-handedly manoeuvred the bike against storm and rain. It was hungry work. I am not sure if the kitchen staff ever noticed the juicy ends of the few missing plucked grapes. In any case, the tips kept on coming, and within a few weeks I went to the camera shop and bought the camera. I always gave my earnings to my parents but was allowed to keep the generous tips. The camera is the same as on Gunther Grass' book. I am sure it was a Brownie Kodak with a strap on top and two view finders. I can still so vividly recall taking my first roll of film. I think it might have been eight photos or perhaps twelve. I took the exposed film spool to the camera shop who told me it would be ready in a week or so. I could hardly wait for them to be in my hands. The photos were poured over for hours. I was totally transfixed by the idea of getting an image to be fixed forever to be looked at over and over again. They had serrated edges as well and in black and white. I took the camera to Australia, and even took photos on the trip over. The boat had a developer on board. My excitement knew no bounds.

This Fallacy of Being Normal.

Here it is again. The co-pilot, Andreas Lubitz, who now seems to have caused the Lufthansa tragedy, was considered by many to be a normal guy, a very friendly man. He was well liked, had a girlfriend, was part of a group of friends, did jogging, and was very friendly. There was nothing in his background that seemed to suggest he would ever do what he finally is alleged to have done; murder 150 innocent people. Perhaps we should be more wary when we hear people say they think they are 'normal' people. Yes, normal, but so was Churchill, who gave a command during WW1, sending thousands to their death on the coast of Turkey in the battle known as Gallipoli. We now have elevated this event to an almost unbelievable act of heroism. It was heroic, but it was also very foolish, well known to be doomed from the start. It was a preventable tragedy. Gallipoli would fall to become the seventh bloodiest campaign of the war, but at the time it had no peer in casualties. That was 'normal', too. Thousands of Australians will go to Turkey this Anzac day to commemorate that tragedy. They will stand there holding candles and remember, 'lest we forget'. Yet, is was a foregone conclusion it would be a massacre on a terrible scale. Within a month of it, Churchill was sacked from the war ministry. It is regarded as one of the biggest stains on the career of Churchill. Yet, the event is now elevated to a level that will surely excite Hollywood movie makers yet again.

And then there was Bush. Perfectly normal, too. Thousands being send to death in the first war of Iraq, all based on a known lie, there were no weapons of mass destruction. Bush knew that, and so did our PM, John Howard. Bush was 'normal'. John Howard, sickeningly normal, too.

Look at how refugees are treated by our respectable government. Thousands of refugees locked up for years on end. This government has said, 'You will never end up living in Australia.' You can rot forever, jump off roofs, go raving mad, but, no matter what you do, we will never allow you your human-ness or any dignity. Yet, our government are peopled by very normal people. Perhaps even normal people are very capable of doing abnormal abysmal deeds!

History seems to bear this out.

Thorn amongst Roses.

Lately, there seems to be always more women around than men. It shows up especially at birthday parties. Of course, in the 65 to 85 age group, many men have carked it. It is a known fact which some women, who might not have rowed quite as well in the gondola of happy marriages, seem to think is fair justice! As soon as one enters the room, and provided one arrives about half an hour later than the agreed time, one gets lots of beseeching female eyes concentrating instinctively on scanning another solitary male, even when accompanied by a female.

The reason could also be that men, instead of calmly dying, don't like social gatherings anymore, and prefer being at home in the recliner watching sport or some pseudo-documentary of bearded Vikings on horseback shooting arrows at random into a stone-walled Yorkshire dale below. Anyway, whatever the reason, in our limited social events, women often outnumber men at least five to one. This was the occasion last night. It was our neighbour's 82nd birthday, to which we were invited. She is a very busy neighbour who knows everybody, having lived in this green spruce and conifer town for most of her life. To be fair, there were four men, and about twelve women. The men were all huddled in a group with the women spread in a semi-circle around the table of food and drinks. I noticed an empty chair between two women and quickly headed for that one.

My other choice would have been to join the men who seemed to know each other. I did not wish to impose on whatever they were so keenly talking about. They often talk about success and achievements. I am more into failures, far more interesting. After settling in and being given a drink I just sat there cross-legged with a smile and feeling confident with my denture firmly in place. The woman on my right made the initiative. She asked where I lived. The woman on the other side joined in. In no time we were talking about what we had done so far in life. I had made a fortunate choice. The woman on my right, who was born before the war, started talking about an experience decades ago. The laws in Australia at the time were still Dickensian. A woman could not get served alcohol in a pub except when seated in the Ladies Parlour. Most times, the favoured drink at that time for ladies in the Ladies Parlour was either a sweet sherry or a shandy, which is a beer watered down with lemonade. Anyway, I soon steered the subject over to the different toilet cultures experienced in overseas countries. This is where the party really got swinging. Fortunately, both women had travelled a lot, and knew the subject of overseas toilets even better than I. I regaled how in those early Australian times the word toilet was never used for women. It was as if women were so delicate, and nice, that they never had a need for ablutions. They just did not go. That's why a toilet for women was referred to as ladies rest rooms, ladies powder rooms, even...in Sydney's Hyde Park, ladies reserves, as if women were rounded up in some kind of South African style Paul Kruger Park behind wire fences.

The woman on my right, Helen, told the story of having driven during the fifties through one of the most isolated parts of Australia, behind Broken Hill, the never-never country of hundreds of miles of dirt road. She was driving straight into the blinding western sun. For hours on end. She finally arrived at Ivanhoe, and headed for the only pub in town wanting a cool beer. The bartender said he would not serve a woman in a public bar. In those times it was just not done, especially not in an outback town, beyond the black stump. She said, I went outside and bawled my eyes out. The bartender relented and said she could have a shandy on the veranda outside, provided she would also eat a meat pie.

Can you imagine? We laughed heartily, and it was a great night.

Methuselah.

I haven't a clue what to say next. Perhaps just start with a word out of the dictionary opened at random; Ohm's Law. The principle that the electric current passing through a conductor is directly proportional to the potential difference. Across it. Well, that's that cleared up. It is amazing, though, how the world of science is so clever to come up with definitions such as Ohm's Law.

My Dad knew about electricity, and I still remember how he tried to explain ohms, volts, amps and other terms relating to electric current. I still don't understand it thoroughly, and am forever stunned by those who do. I can change light bulbs, but even that is getting tricky with those two pinned ceiling light bulbs. They are supposed to last 6000 hours or more but I am sure that that is a commercial honey lure. I don't know how changing those modern light bulbs are experienced by those over ninety. It is frightening how old age is going through the roof. In ten years' time most of us will be over ninety and thousands over one hundred. Has there been a survey or poll on how many of us actually want to get that old? Or has this endless obsession with longevity more to do with getting more money and more consumers over longer periods? Perhaps there are those that want to keep going. I am not sure, but am happy for every day that passes without bouts of intestinal hurry or too spontaneous outbursts of unwarranted optimism.

I see more and more battery operated carts zooming around with the options of shopping bags in front and underneath the occupant. Aisles in shops are now wider, allowing not only for bigger people to shop but also accommodating those over one hundred to shop in electrically driven carts. Forking out the mullah will never stop.

188

One of my granddad's art works (Jan Oosterman).

We went for a walk, but a heatwave made it shorter than normal. We took a break midway in one of those golden-amber stained timber slatted seats overlooking the vivid green of a local cricket field. The seats have been carefully planned underneath giant oak and eucalypts surrounding the pitch. Cricket is like Ohms to me, forever doomed to inaccessibility but the lovely shade is crystal clear, and instantly acceptable. A lady in a loose white cotton dress walking with a same breed of dog as our Milo stopped and chatted while patting both dogs. Her dog, Molly, was eleven and getting less energetic, she told us, also one eye was drooping. A dog is the main lubricant for social interaction, far more so than just us. Without Milo we could be sitting there till Methuselah got home before anyone would come and chat. I suppose that's why people have pets, not just for own pleasure but for others as well. There are those who will take the initiative, and just about talk to anyone without waiting to be approached first. I am always in awe of that skill, and have thought how it is that some can do that without any effort. Fortunately, my Helvi has the nous, and it comes naturally even though she is also somewhat shy. There is a laughter as well that comes without any intent or effort. Perhaps it is confidence!

I was lucky. Never mind the Ohms. I mean the definition; is directly proportional to the potential difference, across it. I still don't get it!

Bees and Salvia.

With the salvia now having taken over most of the garden, bees have descended upon those nodding flowers by the hundreds if not thousands.

After a few days under this wonderful siege, we left them alone. The buzzing noise and hyper activity made Milo, our Jack Russell, nervous. Hanging the washing outside carried an increased risk of getting stung by an over-excited bee, if not covered in salvia pollen as well...Some of the salvia beads of flowers had multiple numbers of bees scrambling for a place inside the flowers. There were disagreements between them, and despite some of the older more wiser bees trying to mediate, try and keep peace, there was nothing much we, as mere humans, could do except pack a couple of bags, some wooden sandals and water, also bread and some mild salami, to seek temporary salvation ourselves. It could well be that salvia's potent hallucinatory substance affects bees in a hostile way. The science is still out on that one. In America there are a few states that have put Salvia on the list of forbidden plants and anyone caught with it could be charged with drug offence. Beware when travelling in the US of using mint in your soup! In any case, we could not pontificate forever about what bees might or might not be capable off. We drove somewhat in an uncertain fashion, but generally following the orange sun in an east-south-westerly direction, and just before dusk managed to get into a place that had a bed with soft pillows but a firm mattress. The building had seen better, more jovial times, but the host was buxom and justifiably friendly as is often the case with soft-fronted women, especially if they have names such as

Maria, Barbara, Josephine and Virginia (but not so much if Gertrude, Kate or Mavis). We asked for a later than usual breakfast, and explained about our reason for departure from our home due to bees being temporarily frenzied by sweet salvia and pollen. She understood and told us the story how her parents had to sell their grand mansion in Chili's Valparaiso and move when their garden became a rehabilitation unit not only for the politically driven mad, infirm and the marital unstable, but also for salvia addicted bees. Her Mum found it easier to counsel the infirm and mad than a frenzied bee. They left for shores named Australia.

We were lucky to have found this place as weekends were usually booked out in advance. They had a cancellation from a couple who were needed for a fund raising to buy a property also taken over by bees. We were somewhat alarmed and uneasy at this notion. Next door was taken by a rather corpulent couple. They seemed to be in a cheerful mood. Each time we met in the corridor they laughed heartily at almost everything we talked about. It was infectious, and I found myself soon laughing spontaneously. The bed and breakfast was guarded by a couple of mastiffs who just gave us a somewhat desultory sniff between our feet to let us pass each time we came home from our walks in a nearby dense forest of tall eucalypts and she oaks. The bees were in profusion here as well, but on the whole friendly and non-intrusive. Of course, we stayed away from the hives that some of the town's folk had put there to possibly supplement meagre incomes, and keep some errant male retirees busy and off the streets. We noticed an elderly, deeply wrinkled man without any protective gear shaking the honey from the combs in a hand driven centrifuge. All he did to calm the bees was smoke a pipe, and with gentle breaths pacified the busy bees. They obviously knew him, and his particular brand of pipe tobacco. We stayed for three nights, and with some sadness said goodbye to our kind host and drove back home. We were pleased to be back, rejuvenated and with some jars of honey. The salvia bees had gone and all was as before, peaceful and sweet.

In Praise of Erectile Dysfunctional Benefits.

It has got me beat, why, when getting older and the morning glory finally in retreat, allowing a bit of a sleep in, that men's obsession with flagging tumescence is called a 'dysfunction'. The scientists in cahoots with sexologists have poured for years over glass test tubes to come up with a solution that will make the ageing male re-born again and cure him from flaccid flesh, drooping donger with dismissive dirges from partners. The expert doctor will now prescribe a pill to try and crank up the tired and ageing engine once again. We all know why doctors' waiting rooms have been seeing more and more men, looking a bit sly, or in some cases shy. The grey haired male heads are now buried in Women's Weekly trying to fill in the remaining clues on the cross words or count the differences in the two pictures. Life hasn't always been easy. All those relationship and marital battles. The kids gone astray up North, bumming around on Noosa's beaches while strumming guitars with silly girls and oafish boys. What about the maintenance and restorations, additions, extensions on houses and costs of kids? All those years of mortgage payments and support on partners and wives long gone?

Oh, that fatal dipping back in one's life, the reminiscing on things gone by, and was all this for the insane drive and biological need for the going of the up and down, and up and down. Is that what has driven us all along in life? Is this why we are sitting here in a doctor's waiting room, all lost and chewed up? Is it to pursue us men forever on?

Better stick to this puzzle making words from rows of letters, see how many I'll get in before seeing the quack and get script on Viagra again. I wonder what the doc does in his old age, no doubt generous in his own prescriptions. Would all this worrying about rigidity in pyjamas next to partners be some giant con to get the pharmaceutical companies out of trouble? I believe there is now a Viagra for women as well; many scientists have worked feverishly on this for a long time. They believe that this new kind of female Viagra makes the blood flow to the pelvic area and it works wonders. Tests, so far done on rats, have shown it to be safely tolerated, and for the pharmaceutical companies a doubling of profits is assured, if we can make normal women feel they have a normal dysfunction as well. Just like us blokes.

There are vague references made to men, as they get older, having vascular problems, smoking or drinking etc., all very normal, and lack of tumescence a result of those chosen life-styles. Never ever, do they say that getting older might mean that things slow down a bit and that the flaccidity problem is a result of healthy ageing and pretty normal? Oh no, around the world, hundreds of millions of men are bombarded with advertisements on how normal it is to have ED, but -and this is the triumph of money over common sense- it is a DYSFUNCTION and therefore not normal. Millions don't want to be feeling they have a dysfunction, and hence the queue to the doctors and the handing over of billions to the merchants of Viagra, Cialis, Ram Rods, Pole Vaulters and others. It seems that the mature man perhaps ought to take matter in own hand, step back sceptically and re-consider the issues a bit more thoroughly.

Could it be that advancing age is blessed with well-hidden benefits of not having to be driven by those ridiculous up and downs, up and downs again? It is not as if, afterwards, one ends up in Kalgoorlie or Vienna. No, we are still in the same spot and our partner will soon be snoring. The Viagra now is calling for a revenge, but will settle for a solid bout of thirty six hours of indigestion. Gee, what rotten luck. The Sudoku has been done in the May 2002 edition of New Idea magazine. Don't doctors ever think that patients might like something a bit more recent?

Just a good cuddle is what we are really wanting more than this struggle with rigid or sloppy bits, and being dependent on a pill. It's our entire fault, the stupid chasing of something that has gone, changed for something else, youth that is gone, thankfully gone! Who would want to go through all that again? Surely by now, we could be looking forward to at least not having to worry about erections at bedtime and forgetting the Viagra. We finally have the house paid, plenty of knives and forks, all the things at last in the right place, made a few friends and got it made, with pictures of smiling grandkids as proof. The ride-on mower and two door fridge.

And afterwards, that glass of red, post dinner and on the comfy settee with partner in opposite armchair, nothing doing, not TV or Vid, nor noisy kids or tumbling dryer and dishwasher. Just be sitting there. How glorious. That's it; we are fed up with being taken as a sucker, enough is enough. We have done our heaving and hoisting for pleasure, procreation and progeny, more than enough for the time being. Put it all to pasture for a year or so, go for hugs and kisses, smell the roses and enjoy time left. No worries, yippee!

Doctor will see you now. Yes, doc; I have got such a persistent corn...

Eve's Apple. Was It Dodgy?

It is always good to know that in writing you just have to know the first word. The rest usually follows from then. I decided my first word for the day to be 'apple'. It is round in shape and when spoken out loud, sounds evenly balanced between vowels and consonants. Of course, the logical word to follow after 'apple' could well be Granny Smith, or even the rosy Lady Pink. I thought to try and associate Eve to the apple.

You sometimes wonder how a modern version of Adam and Eve would turn out. The eager acceptance by Adam of Eve's apple was the beginning of the end, really. I mean, the apple was just a decoy for a many folded love secret kept well hidden by a cunning Eve. She knew it would be irresistible to Adam, transfixed as he was from then on to her litheness while sliding from the tree in that Garden of Eden. It worked its charm but with devastating results. It became complicated. I mean, who would have thought it would result in the painting of the Sistine Chapel's ceiling by Michael Angelo? Was Eve all that innocent and still virginal with that offer of an apple, or was that apple loaded with venom, spite and revenge? A trick to get more little Adams and Eves roaming that lush park of flowing creeks, some sparse shrubs and sharp thistles. To lure him within her, sate him, empty to oblivion and so much nothingness?

On the other hand, did Adam not see the serpent with glistening eyes also slithering from that same tree? He could have given the apple to the snake instead of grabbing it himself. He had a choice! It is all now so complicated and so much water under the bridge. I have also yielded to temptation and gone over to white bread. The birdseed whole meal version has lost out. Forgive me, Daddy, I am nothing but a failure! I also broke a promise to take on smoking again at sixty five having given it up some decades earlier. It was the only thing that I could think of as a reward for giving it up. I failed a few times but none so badly as not having kept my promise to take it up again when I turned sixty five. It is too late now. No going back or suffering regrets. Je ne regrette rien.

Going back to lithesome Eve. I would have cut the apple and offered her half. Furthermore, I would look Eve in the eye and, after a few communal bites, while sauntering around the garden, offering a few words of my own, I would ask her kindly, your place or mine…?

A Horse, a Horse, a Kingdom for a Horse… (Steak)

There are so many different strokes for different folks it makes a mockery of absolute truth or common sense, or even us keeping a semblance of being sane. As some say; what is grist to the mill is porridge for the porkers. Who can't but be amused over the shocking revelations that horse meat has been eaten in Britain? People were seen choking on their tripe and tripping over their chokos. What, eating horse? We are English, don't you know? Cameron was keen in pointing out the moral repugnance of having been dudded by the French in meat being horse meat instead of real meat, the holy cow. I am sure many were also outraged by having eaten horse, never mind morals of eating any animal. There is growing outrage, and of course, its les frogs who are to blame. What insult, with 'les chevaux' being mixed into our beloved frozen hamburger mince. What will the neighbours think?

The irony must be crystal clear to many of the non-Anglo world that in a country where just about everyone is brought up on horse racing, betting and punting, that the eating of horses is seen as abhorrent, close to eating babies or to boarding out children to schools. (Hold onto your horses, we do that lovingly.) We all know that horses are not allowed to be whipped anymore and much is made to prove we don't, with lots of TV footage of horses being stroked and even kissed (on the flaring nostril after having made a packet for the owner and the punters). Surely, that's proof of our love for horses!

Yes, but what about the proof that horse racing is cruel and not far removed from Espanol bull fighting or Indonesian cock-fighting. The animals are manically competing against each other, and when their chance of winning is beyond hope they will end up in paddocks, hopefully looked after by caring owners but many also with enlarged hearts, lungs and tissue damage. It is estimated that about 60% of horses trained for racing end up at the knackery well before their natural lives would have expired. That's right, next time you open a tin of Pal dog food, look deep inside, you are looking at Beaux Hoofs or Triple Ur Dollar. Many also are so psychologically damaged, too nervous and flighty, unfit for casual riding around the paddock. We also know that many are damaged during racing with torn muscles, ligaments and tendons.

Look, having come from Holland I have eaten horse meat as well. Mea Culpa to all horse lovers. It was one of Mum's bitter disappointments that David Jones' delicatessen in Australia did not sell smoked prosciutto from horse meat. 'Oh, no, we don't sell horse meat,' she was told. My Mum blithely unaware of the cultural sensitivity, answered, 'Oh, you should try it, it is sooo delicious... mmm...' She smacked her lips. The shop girl disappeared, fainted behind the counter. I don't think the French, Dutch or Italians love horses any less than the Brits or Irish but make less of a fuss when eating them. The Dutch are more likely not to eat sheep. Those poor little lambs etc. It is strange isn't it, with that lovely children's song with Little Bo Peep that it hasn't filtered down in Britain to then also not eat lamb.

Different strokes etc... and so it goes on. The more one learns about people the more I like my lentils and stroke my Milo. Our incorrigible Jack Russell.

My Top Ten of Erotic Imaginings with Vasectomy as Best Friend.

What Dr Barbara Simcock doesn't know about the male genitalia isn't worth talking about. At the last count in 2005, she had done over 16,000 vasectomies and still counting. That is a minimum of 32,000 testes she has peered at, and pondered about. An amazing feat. I hope she sleeps soundly. If anyone is deserving of a

Dame/Knighthood, surely she is. She looked at mine in 1972 when it -the vasectomy, not the testicles- was still a bit of a novelty. A commercial TV station, Channel 9, interviewed me live afterwards on the telly, interspersed with advertisements for Cadbury Marsh bars. 'How is your performance now?' the smirking girl asked. According to Helvi, who watched the interview, I visibly shrunk and leaned back in my chair. 'Oh, very nice, thank you,' I answered ever so politely.

My Mum, previously a devout believer in 'letting the little ones come' was surprisingly tolerant having watched the TV segment of her son's interview. She even wished the procedure would have been available during her years of green meadows fertility and almost yearly pregnancies. I am not sure if Dad would have volunteered. They were different times. Dr. Barbara wished me well after I walked out of the Family Planning Clinic, testes bandaged securely, gave me a packet of coloured (and flavoured) condoms, and urged me to 'do it as often as you like. Clearing all systems of life sperm is important,' she added. Also, 'You need to give a sample in six weeks to determine how diligent you have been, and that you are ready for a lifetime of sex without worrying about unwanted pregnancies.' I couldn't wait. Surely, the advice 'as often as you like' also needed an equally enthusiastic partner, unless of course, a helping hand was allowed in the clearing of the 'vasa deferentia'. I was given the address of the pathologist that would determine my sample to see if everything was ready for a full steam conjugal trip around the world for ever and ever.

I don't want to get too medical. I'll keep it short and to the point. Those who have followed so far, but who are likely to get upset about explicit sexual references, have the chance to leave now or look askance and think of Brussels sprouts, or depending on cultural backgrounds, of Spanish Chorizos. After a hectic six weeks and looking pale, I wearily made my way to the City pathologist on the bus from Balmain. It was the 401. The girl at the counter smiled friendly and supportively, gave me a small glass jar, and led me to a room. 'You will have plenty of time, the next client won't be here till another hour. Please, you can lock the room behind you,' she added. She smiled again, but not too much so. Just supportive and so typical of her gender. No fuss...

The first thing that struck me of the room was the total lack of a romantic ambience. I thought it would be softly furnished with a warm pink glow. The wall was adorned with a horrible print of a ghoulishly green Egyptian Pharaoh woman, which one sees in op-shops. Nothing but a few magazines and some shelving, on top of which was a packet of Kleenex tissues. What was I supposed to do? I sat down in the Parker chair feeling dejected and not at all keen, staring at my little glass jar. What had I got myself into, and what will the girl at the desk think when I hand over my empty jar? I perused the magazines. They were full of the most provocative and beckoning ladies. What I thought were advertisements for chicken wings turned out to be close ups of shaven genitals. On top of all that, was I going to be unfaithful in this hour of such desperation (and of which was no return) to chicken wings? I looked at my watch. Thirty five minutes had passed already and to make things worse, a couple of male voice were outside my door. Are they queuing up now? I panicked. It was all still so flappery foppery.

But then, I relaxed and thought, surely you can do it. Something was awakening, a kind of doing it for your country and the over-population scourge together with a lust to prove to the girl behind the counter, I was still a man. I took action by first moving away from the Pharaoh woman's gaze on the wall. Resolute and determined, I decided to recall my most and best top ten in the hit parade of sexual imaginings. The ones that withstood the test of time, over and over again. I think it was number six with the heaving and sighing and languid look that IT rose to the occasion. My little glass jar tilted at the ready, was now ever so willing and able. There were still sixteen minutes left and I relaxed to the point of, I might as well make the most of it, heroically relishing the lovely tingling

creeping up my spine and, while recklessly easing off a little, took my time and gave helping hand a bit of earned rest, only to resume my previous momentum, except a little faster and more urgent now. I unlocked the door, and triumphantly handed over my discretely wrapped in Kleenex tissues compliant glass jar to the smiling girl. I had still seven minutes left. I could almost have used the extra time for a post conjugal nap as well. But there was another client waiting.

A Nostalgic Look Back At My Colonoscopy.

When I wrote the vasectomy piece a few day ago I did not know that I would be in for spamming e-mails trying to flog pills promising to 'Enlarge your man meat' and 'Make her scream for more of you', followed this morning with the cheery, 'Satisfy even the most insatiable nymphomaniac with your relentless sexual power!' At my age, I just enjoy a warm milk and spoonful of honey stirred in. The last thing I would want is a screaming nymphomaniac lunging for my manhood. She might have trouble finding it now! It brought back memories of my colonoscopies some years back. I don't know why. Perhaps the images of 'man-meats' and most male porn, dedicated to images of turkey wattles and inner bicycle tyres, has that effect on me. It turns the mind to the opposite of erotica, perhaps as a calmative, antidote, or kind of army administered bromide in tea, to keep hands above the blankets. Hence, a look now back on my colonoscopy. It is a grey day and raining relentlessly.

The colonoscopy was performed by a good and fully qualified endoscopist/doctor. I don't know what drives anyone to become an investigator of colons. The same might well be asked of those that put down words in a certain order. The writer also puts up with semi-colons but is lucky to get a single dollar for his efforts. At least the inspector of colons gets paid handsomely. He might come home to a lovely wife (or husband), gets served up a nice lamb chop with English spinach. He can relax, and regale to spouse about his terrific colonoscopies performed during the day. He might be tired but has done his job well. He knows that. The writer of words has to stumble in the dark. It is not as clear cut as a polyp post polypectomy. He has a feeling, but feelings are often strange bedfellows. How words feel can change. They are not set in concrete. Definitions of words are there, but as soon as you put another word next to it, it changes. A rose at dawn is withered at dusk. He hopes for the best but as luck has it, he/she has one arrow, unfailing and unwavering. It is the enjoyment of it. So, in a way, the colon investigator and word writer might both be as necessary. In fact, both might be symbiotic.

It was during my second last colonoscopy. The nurse asked me to draw my knees up higher. 'Doctor needs good access,' she murmured. I obliged, I knew the score, and was on first name basis with the good doctor. I woke up during his attempt to remove yet another obstinate polyp. The pain was somewhat greater than the tranquilizer. As I woke, I looked at the screen, and in my drugged and confused state thought I was having a look at turkey wattle inner tube bicycle porn. The horror, the horror! Fortunately it was my own bowel, the very end of it.

I woke up in bed, and after an hour or so was rewarded by a kind nurse with a nice ham and cheese sandwich with a lovely lime jelly as desert. I was so hungry!

A Perfect Place, Amsterdam?

Where to settle in a place that is perfect? A place that meets all one's wishes, expectations and needs. A community of men and friendly beast, that lifts spirit and soul, offers shelter and fulfils the most. A Mecca of sun and dreams! A final garden seat in which to rest, repose, restore, revitalize life's joys, offer an escape from the hovels of hurts. I would like rivulets with small stones and flowing waters, frogs a-croaking and barking dogs with visions of fleeting ducks. Is there such a place and can it be found? We lived for very long periods in few places, countable on the fingers of one hand.

Our main departure from having permanently lived in Australia were the three years spent in Holland. It was between 1973 and 1976. We have very fond memories of that period. A lovely very old farm-house, a thatched roof and giant oak beams spanning the walls of a very large living room. We had a couple of sheep, an obstinate Shetland pony, and brown chickens all on about two and a half acres. In many ways it was idyllic. But, we did go back!

Now, in final years still left to live, we again dream about possible places to explore. The kids have gone, and our grandkids are getting ready to tackle life. We love and wish them all the best. Retirement was meant for us. The time is ours and we can afford to be somewhat selfish. 'May the devil take the hindmost' is an expression that seems to occur with greater frequency. A final plunge in unknown pools, a journey to 'the perfect place'. Of course, deep down we know that it does not exist but in dreams alone. The frangipani flowers but only in warm enough climes where tulips and daffodils will not.

The obstinate Shetlander and foal at our farm.

Yesterday, I took the luxury of dreaming what it would be like to once again pack up and try a dip into the unknown. The unknown being explored in real estate of Amsterdam, specifically its beautiful centre. You know, something around the Westertoren or indeed in the Jordaan. It would be so nice!

Own Home Of Fibro Asbestos Cement.

It was to be the fulfilment of Australia's promise to migrants; 'You will end up owning your own home'. In

Australia, dreams and aspirations are made of working towards own home. It worked for my parents but they were also, unwittingly, working towards a strong possibility of owning their own coffin in the bargain. It sounds a bit grim, therefore let me explain. Before coming to Australia, as far as we were concerned, we owned a home. True, there was a lull in the event during WW2 when living in own home was often precarious with reckless sorties of planes flying overhead dropping incendiary devices that were decidedly anti home. But, by and large, people lived in own homes. Actually, and speaking strictly, we did not own home in as much as it was possible to own a shirt or underpants, but we did own a home in the sense of having a secure roof over our heads that was indisputably ours. No one ever even thought of a possible owning of a pile of bricks and timber like you did when you bought a shirt or underpants. Most people lived and died in a home whose bricks and walls were owned by the government of the country or the city that one lived in. It was never thought of otherwise, and it never occurred that we were at risk of not being able to live there as long as we wanted. Titles of ownership were mostly unheard of.

After my parents' arrival in Australia, owning a home was almost right from the start the main conversation between many new arrivals. First, you bought own block of land, and this would be followed with building own house. This is what drove almost every migrant and was soon seen as the raison d'être for having migrated in the first place. First, my Dad was perplexed by this new type of living, whereby one had to buy a roof over one's head. Why was it so different from Holland where a roof was considered something you rented for life, and never worried about having to buy it? It was all a bit of a puzzle, but soon 'toute la famille' were taken in by the fervour of the own home rush, busy with working with getting at least a deposit together. The term deposit was also something totally unheard of, as were people called 'Real Estate agents.' Dutch migrants that we met in this frenzied atmosphere of own homes got together with my parents at weekends, and talked almost exclusively about deposits and estate agents, rates of interest on loans and The Dutch Building society that would give loans.

The memory of Schubert's Lieder and my soft breasted Margo now seemed so far away, unobtainable forever. Separated by oceans of dried salt tears.

'How's your deposit going?' was so much more of the essence now?

In a very quick time, with all the Oostermans capable of working with lots of overtime being paid at double or triple at weekend rates, a deposit was saved. Exploratory train trips were made to many different suburbs of outer lying Sydney to investigate own block of land. Those trips were also sometimes made with a Real-Estate agent. My Dad thought it such a strange term. 'Are there 'Un-real Estate agents as well?" he would flippantly ask the agent?

At the late fifties, Shire-Councils closed an eye to migrants living on blocks of land with a garage on it. It was euphemistically called a temporary dwelling. My Mum spotted an advertisement of such a temporary dwelling in Revesby. Revesby then was on the edge of Sydney's civilization, still un-sewered, but with a pub in the making, and most importantly, was on a rail-line with a rail-way station, schools and a church, even a fish and chips shop! I have never forgotten the salty potato scallops wrapped in The Sun newspaper. My Dad paid the feverishly debated deposit, and after a few weeks the land and its asbestos sheeted garage was ours. Now, this is where the possibility of own home with the possibility of own coffin creeps in. Even as early as the late forties and fifties, cases of a mysterious and deadly serious disease started coming in, especially from workers who worked in the Wittenoom asbestos mines of Western Australia.

http://en.wikipedia.org/wiki/Wittenoom,_Western_Australia

However, the action on the link between asbestos and the 1948 diagnosed asbestosis was delayed and deliberately ignored. In fact, during the period that already had scores of victims of asbestosis, Australia was building hundreds of thousands of houses sheeted externally -and sometimes internally as well- with fibro cement asbestos sheeting. It was thought by bonding the dangerous asbestos with cement it would be a safe and cheap building product. We first lived in the 8 by 4 meters of unpainted and unlined asbestos sheeted temporary dwelling, and then for another eighteen years in a small house made from the same asbestos fibro sheeted home. None of us succumbed to the dreadful asbestos induced cancer Mesothelioma. We were lucky. Not so were those having died so far, or the untold who will continue to die in the future. A sad price to pay for own home.

In 1948, Dr. Eric Saint, a Government Medical Officer, wrote to the head of the Health Department of Western Australia. He warned of the dust levels in the mine and mill, the lack of extractors, and the dangers of asbestos with risk of asbestosis. He advised that the mine would produce the greatest crop of asbestosis the world has ever seen. You can see why I now feel that the dream of own home could well have been a very nasty and expensive coffin for our parents and their children. How come Australia doesn't provide alternative accommodation to all who still live in asbestos containing fibro cement sheeted homes and give compensation to all the sufferers?

The Possibility of Fracking Governments.

Many eminent scientists say that when you put pressure on something the result is often a release of pent-up energy. It is now used to release gas locked up in rock formations. It is called fracking. Geologists come home tired and their wives now ask, 'Did you do some good fracking today, dear?' 'Go and frack yourself' is an expression waiting to raise its head in parlance of the progressive world of slinky board riders and depressed gloomy hoodie wearers. I bet you it will take over from the 'awesome' and 'oh my god'. I think stuff like that has now sunk into the furnace of lost expressions, the same as bodgie and widgie many decades ago. It was used during the period when as a teenager I used to linger around Parramatta Delinquent Girls Home. Friday night was curler-night. I remember seeing girls in trains wearing curlers! Men used to perve on the Pix magazine with girly photos showing knees and totally naked feet.

I have just brushed up my very limited knowledge on Islam and ISIS with all that goes with it; I can't say I am much wiser. Previous knowledge about the Middle East did not go much further than Ali Baba and forty thieves. On the way over from Holland our boat stopped at Port

Said where we all went off the ship. I was fifteen and bought a fez and a small whip used for camel driving. I kept those mementoes for years. Now they are lost the same as those past popular expressions. Forever gone! I do know that bombing always ends up killing. With the latest beheading, no doubt the reaction will be more bombing, more killing, and more incomprehension by many, not least myself. Isis seems to have unlimited funding and an expert PR machinery going for it. Perfectly English translations of their web-sites and IT magazines beamed and downloaded all over. It is there within seconds, as was the latest beheading video, done by the same man speaking in a thick London accent.

I don't know what goes on. The last major conflicts in Vietnam, Iraq and Afghanistan were all undertaken at the behest of the US. All three conflicts seemed to have achieved nothing but hordes of refugees with endlessly ongoing murderous campaigns. We were lied to by our governments as never before. Vietnam did not result in hordes of yellow peril. Iraq did not have weapons of mass destruction. Afghanistan with the Taliban were America's friends during the period they were fighting the Russians.

And now... again, Australia goes to another war. And talking about expressions, our Government calls this... not going to a war, but... 'A humanitarian MISSION'! Can you believe it?

How Did It Get To 50?

Our children in Holland 1973

A good friend left a message on our answering service yesterday congratulating us on fifty years of marriage. How did this come about? It only seems like yesterday. We had totally forgotten. We have never stood still reflecting much on wedding anniversaries. We do of course remember each other's birthdays. Christmases, too, come and go. The important thing is to get up each day and celebrate that marvellous event more than the one yearly or one in fifty years event.

Here is how!

'How did you sleep?' 'Very good, how about you?' 'Oh, very good, just went to toilet just once, I think it was at 4.30, or no, it might have been a bit earlier, perhaps 3.30. I slept very deeply again afterwards, like an angel.' 'You don't look like an angel, get a haircut today, you look wild, more like a Hottentot.' 'Yes, but then I have to wash my hair, take a shower, too.' 'So what? Have you got a problem, taking a shower?' 'No, not that, but it is still too early.' 'You are not too early with being banal.' 'Yes, I know, feel free! It is not too late. Many would find you very attractive, and you've got lovely eyes.' 'Get #u&&et.' 'How's the coffee, dear? Strong enough?' 'Yes, it is a nice one today.' 'It's Lavazza, ground. We are on the last kilo.' 'OK, next when it is on special we get two kilos again.' 'Yes, at Farmers Market.' 'I had a stomach cramp during the night. I might have eaten too much of the hummus.' 'Yes, I noticed you were hoeing into it last night with the crackers, too. Were you hungry?' 'You're a very healthy girl, you eat more than me!' 'Not as healthy as you will be, emptying the red again.' 'Well, you know after the drive from Sydney, one needs a bit of a relaxation.' 'You say that every night'. 'Yes, I know, but we don't take any medication, you've got to have something! We don't smoke, don't take any medication, live frugally, still have most of our teeth. So what if we drink a bit?' 'True, dear, especially if it is a good one.' 'I might go upstairs and check the blogs. Have you looked yet?' 'No, I haven't. I am still tired.' 'Oh, there you go again, meckering as usual. Cheer up.' 'I am cheery, have you looked at the lilies, another one has opened up, there are now three open'. 'Yes, I noticed, make another coffee and take it upstairs.' 'All right dear, I will.'

And that is the answer to how fifty years have passed. (And all too quickly)

Growing Older: The Challenge of the Ages.

Australia's population is ageing. The insurance companies have cottoned on. Death is stalking our airwaves as never before. Let's hope the government pays as much attention to our older generations.

We all know we will be lucky to get out of this alive. Most of us live as if it will continue forever, whooping it up at Ikea, David Jones, or Harvey Norman, spending big on items that will most likely cark it well before we do. It's when the kids have left, mortgages put to rest, and the credit card finally paid off that it begins to dawn on some of us that there might be more to life than living. It is called getting old. I think the canny insurance companies know it, too. We used to be bombarded by detergent and suds soap TV advertisements with the young housewife swanning about the brick veneer singing the praise of a bacteria-free kitchen and odourless toilet. Not anymore! Death is stalking our airwaves as never before.

As soon as the evening news has finished, with the help of two or even three accompanying news readers (all laughing and spreading good cheer, no matter how many bombings or catastrophes have occurred), we get to advertisements even more serious than the news, urging us to get a good and solid funeral plan. I think the insurance companies have put on their thinking caps, and after viewing the statistics on an ever increasing army of the old and ageing, are honing into one of the most lucrative markets of them all. This is the funeral market, a road of no return, especially not by customers hardly likely to ask for a refund. They usually show a couple of oldies, with the audacity of being always so happy. The reason soon becomes clear. As they cavort on a lovely green lawn with kids chasing a ball, the wife proudly regales to the viewers how her loving husband has bought into a terrific funeral insurance plan, all for less than the cost of a weekly coffee latte. They are seen wandering off into the dusk of a golden sunset, secure in the knowledge that coffins are at the ready and fully paid for. It must be nice to be so secure, almost as if the cremation retort is already set on low or 'stand-by'. Then there is the oddity of so many wishing to go back to; where do we come from'? Why? What drives so many to dig up the past in the skeletal annals of our ancestry in birth, marriage and death certificates in the forlorn hope of finding a famous figure in their background? For most it seems a murderer or prostitute is all they can hope to find... We soon might well be skeletons ourselves. What is the hurry?

The ageing population is now in the majority, and it is amongst the elderly that the fairer sex now outshines the grumpy masculine ones. They used to be called the weaker sex, but make no mistake, women have always been the stronger ones. They just used to assuage the male in believing they were. Just have a look at the shopping centres. It becomes obvious. Even a cursory look around the dairy divisions of the supermarkets you see those resolute women leading their husbands around. The ageing males seem to totter and become helplessly dependent on choosing anything, let alone make a choice in low cholesterol margarine or low-fat, pre-sliced cheeses. Those males seem to wander off into a world of pondering and reflection of things gone by. The woman sticks to the issues of the present and steers the marital boat into calmer waters with the rudder set solidly, steering it steadily forward and well away from marital storms and tempests.

Gas bills and council rates are all paid in time. He is reminded more often now than before to put his socks in the laundry basket and take timely showers. There is still lovely food and nice conversations with friends and family, but perhaps it might be best to avoid rabbiting about 'the good old days', a sure sign of really getting old. I drive my grandchildren to despair and back home to Sydney when going on about the cost of petrol in the old days, or how we used to be enthralled by Franquin the Magician being as hilarious as an event as could be. Don't ever mention Jules Verne or having danced a foxtrot. We should have the wisdom to age as innocuously as possible and leave the young to their world of iPod, iPad, tablets or apps, and console yourself that they too will succumb to a similar fate.

You will all be lucky to get out of this alive, I tell them. They look a bit bewildered when I say this. My wife tells them, 'Don't take him seriously. Your granddad is going gaga.' I can still put on my own socks and walk rather briskly, so my lovely wife tells me. Many of my friends get e-readers with adjustable fonts, stronger spectacles, cataract removal operations and hearing aids. Some get about on electric wheelchairs scooting up and down the streets or around shopping centres. Most of us stay clear of those large Meccas for consumption we visited so frequently when younger. The times are different but totally ours, finally. Most of us hope that whoever gets into government will reckon with the rapidly growing army of the elderly. A mighty force. I would not like to face a golf club-swinging group of cranky old men nor resolute women armed by sharpened umbrellas. Watch out Kevin or Tony, and now Malcolm Turnbull, we too matter. No more shortage of well-trained staff in aged facilities or stories of dreadful abuse. If governments can afford 'gaming' palaces they can fund care for the elderly.

This journey is still ongoing. But, just in case of an early demise; keep off the grass!

Home Alone.

Mention the word table (tavola) to an Italian and the implications are clear: family, food, laughter, and above all, the excitement of conversation. The word 'tavola' could easily bring tears to any red-blooded Italian, having been away too long from home. But, mention the word 'table' to an Australian and someone might ask: Ikea, or have you inherited a Parker Table?

(This, of course, is not the only difference between Aussies and the European or other nationals. But, as they often say, Viva La Difference!)

A curious form of isolating oneself, at times, from the outside world, persists here more than anywhere else that I know of. Perhaps the words, Own Home, demonstrate this difference. Am I right in thinking that those two little words would conjure up for Australians what the word 'tavola' does for the Italian? The words 'Own Home' for us Australians is the need for a world of absolute 'privacy'. Perhaps, to our Anglo forbearers, Own Home, was their castle. Up with the drawbridge and just in case of anything or anyone unwanted, they had the back up of a moat to keep out intruders, including any unannounced visitors. While the drawbridge and moat have gone, we have substituted them with the paling fence, and now the impenetrable colour bond aluminium partition fence, blocking even the remotest chance of seeing a neighbour, or worse, a neighbour seeing us. Some 'own homes' now have total block-out metal electric window shutters. Perhaps in the future they will do away with the need to have any windows at all.

The Train to Rookwood.

Woody Allen's answers in an interview with a journalist some years ago were quirky, witty, and to the point. His best was towards the end when he seemed to reject the notion that getting older equates to the getting of wisdom. On the questions of why we are here and what the point of life was, he remained modestly unsure. Whatever he gained through all the years, he would gladly have exchanged it all for "...wiping thirty-five years off the calendar," adding, with a distant look, that he would probably make the same mistakes all over again.

This might have been a bit tongue in cheek, but made me think how much profit there is in getting older. Surely, there has to be some reward for having survived all the misery and sadness of having lived through so much uncertainty with the many difficulties. It is not unreasonable to assume that one becomes better with the passing of years at coping with some of the misfortunes and events that could, with foresight, have been avoided, and that the benefits of getting older begets us the wisdom to not repeat errors and mistakes into the future. We plod on with expectations of improvements, and hope that with age, we will undoubtedly get rewards for the courage, determination and resilience in having cobbled something out of our lives. When enough time has lapsed, we can have the luxury of reflectively, taking stock, and doing the accounts, with hopefully finding out that, by and large, we stayed the course, and that we had achieved the things that we sat out to reach with the positives having outweighed the negatives.

When young, and bursting with enthusiasm and raging hormones, we recklessly hurled ourselves into the future, taking and accepting risks, relationships and partners all at once and with wild abandonment. We brazenly and bravely fought to make our mark. Nothing would stop us. We blindly believed that hard work and enterprise would ensure a stake in prosperity and much goodness, not just for ourselves, but also for our offspring and others. Deposits would be made on house and car. Schools for kids would be booked years in advance. Inexorably with the passing of a few more years, we would reap rewards by climbing into even better and bigger houses with more bathrooms. We have larger cars with DVD players hooked from the back seat for kids to watch Shrek when driving somewhere and anywhere.

Did we also not take in our stride the misfortune of family life gone off at a tangent or even astray, with lives, like forgotten letters in the drawer, damaged or lost through accident, illness and inherited gene, or the scourge of modern age, addiction to evil substance?

With the advance of years beyond the half century, we fully expect that wisdom and experience will guide us to calmer waters, and ease us into a nice and comfortable latter part. With the luck of robust health and benefit of not smoking anymore finally reaching old age. We paid our dues and the mortgage man is now finally sated. The credit card we will keep on sailing with, just in case of the unforeseen, the failing of car or broken and worn washer-dryer, a trip to Venice, or even Chile's Santiago.

Having steamed through that post mortgage -and for some, post marriage- years, we have now travelled to the beginning of an advanced age with the cheerful Senior Newsletter and Senior's card in the post. The Senior Newsletter has holidays for the advanced seniors at Noosa and a plethora of advertisements for those handy battery operated electric little carriages with shopping trays at the back. Are we to zoom in and out of shopping centres soon, using ramps up and down? With the sheer numbers appearing on footpaths now, it won't be long until there could be outbreaks of motorized wheelchair-rage?

I suppose there has been a major drop-out of readers now. Who wants to get ahead that far?

Please, don't get impatient. Just hang in here for another eighty or so words, when at age 80, we are almost there, indeed, we have arrived. How did we fare? It is time now to have one more go at something, perhaps golf for the very fit or, dread the thought, bowling with cricket gear all in pristine white and with men wearing neatly pressed pantaloons but suspiciously bulging when bending to bowl!

Once more, we listen, hear and hum the forlorn, 'Le Piano du Pauvre'.

I am nothing

I exist

Only in the generous eyes of others

Somehow, with The Train to Rookwood now at station, we have so far stumbled, bumbled but stoutly plotted on. Time has finally arrived, with casket to carriage, no time for regret.

Death

Inaccessible

Even to memory

Appears and goes away

With a scull

For a nod

The Train to Rookwood.

Poems by friend Bernard Durrant.

First Dates and Concrete Bras.

I don't know about you, but first dates have a habit of infringing on memories as nothing else will. The catastrophes of life certainly include my attempts at romance many years ago as a young migrant that had just arrived in Australia. On top of having a strong guttural accent and no car, the hopelessness of my situation can well be imagined by some of you. My wheels at the time were a Lambretta scooter. I was also the proud secretary of the Parramatta Scooter club; motor bikes not allowed. My position of power allowed me to get my brother to come on a few treasure hunt trips, even though he had a single cylinder Norton 500cc motor bike. I soon found out that my chances of dating a Sheila would improve greatly if I had a car. This is where my 1949 Ford Single Spinner came into being. It was light blue with leather seats back and front, and used oil almost as much as petrol.

I already found out through bitter experience that just to get a girl to dance was fraught with difficulties. There were so many men and so few girls willing to dance with nerds and reffos (refugees). The Ford V8 had to achieve what Dutch panache could not. The trick was to let it be known that you had car. The fifties and sixties dance places in Sydney numbered the Trocadero in George Street, which is now a gaudy cinema complex, and Vic's Cabaret at Strathfield. Both had different bands and ambiences. It was also the period of TV serials Bonanza and 77 Sunset Strip. In one of those was a character called Little Joey, or was it Cookie, who was forever combing his hair while posing at a rakish angle to the movie camera. There were thousands of pretend Joeys, Cookies and James Dean lookalikes and the competition was fierce. My trump-card had to be the Ford V8. I tried with copious Brylcreme bouffant coiffure to emulate a mixture of all three of the TV stars. As I was already 6ft I could not be 'little Joey', but with a little practice might just convey a hint of that same mysterious masculinity and excitement.

The Pride of Erin was the only dance ensuring blokes of at least getting one dance in. The multi mirrored ball hanging from the ceiling was throwing fascinating effects all around, and as was the norm then, Sheilas with bee-nest hairstyles and hooped skirts with steel ironed petty coats holding them out with budding breasts safely encased in conical shaped concrete bras shackled at the back with rustproof buckles (pressed against a lucky hand when dancing), would be coyly seated on one side, and shiny eyed, horny and well brilliantined blokes on the opposite. No matter how the girls twirled and swirled while dancing, no body parts would ever bounce up and down or move, perhaps, just in case male desires would get aroused unnecessarily or even involuntary. Bras and other attire would resist the pesky hand, even of a Houdini.

This Pride of Erin was a dance whereby partners would change at every swirl or so, hence refusals by girls were kept at a minimum. You would have to be legless if you did not get a dance in.

My Waterloo had arrived. The band struck up a cheery, 'What's the Matter with Kids Today?' Everyone rushed forward and I got a 'Yes, please' at the request for a dance. After changing with different girls, I got one with a friendly smile and kind look. I only had seconds, so, suppressing my accent as much as possible, and flicking my hair back with practiced Cookie nonchalance, asked for a date the following Saturday. Unbelievably, she agreed. That Saturday, I turned up with a brand new Van Heusen shirt and polished Ford V8 and, after a thorough inspection by a very large Dad, we drove to Gosford, taking in culture and the home place of the famous artist, William Dobell, at Wangi Wangi. We also drove to a small place, Woy Woy. The previous week there had been a Willy Willy (aboriginal for Tornado) at Woy Woy. For an unfathomable reason I included the devastation and mayhem there on our itinerary. She was very quiet, but kept saying, 'Oh, how nice,' interspersed with, 'Thank you,' which at least was something. It was a difficult day, and I took care going up any steep hill, to take it easy on the V8, not wishing the burning of oil and blue smoke to spoil things.

At the end of the day and drive, I took her back to her formidable Dad and she thanked me generously again. There was not an encore, ever. Years later, having outgrown the Trocadero, Vic's cabaret, Brylcreme and the Ford V8, I decided to go to Europe and get a proper job. I went to work in a bank, went to Austria, where I met my present partner on the ski slopes at Lienz, in Ost Tyrol, Austria. A lucky and very fortuitous break.

The Restless Book Searcher. A Short Story.

The sun was at its highest this time of the year. A man carrying a swag and back-pack was seen walking the deserted streets. His cattle dog cleverly walked in the limited shade that the walker was still casting. The merciless heat was parching the dust which was as much in need of water, and as thirsty as the man and his dog. He finally arrived at a small shop which had a 'Tip-Top bread' sign hanging from its awning. On the shop window there were plastered a variety of signs, including one on 'Big Ben' pies, also a poster of Camel Cigarettes featuring a goggled fighter pilot in his cockpit with 'nerves of steel' and a 'Vincent's APC Headache' powder advertisement. Even though the torn and battered fly screen door was slightly ajar, it had a 'closed' sign facing any possible customer on the outside. The owner of this shop had lost the will to turn the sign around to 'open' a long time ago, and anyhow, with the fly-screen refusing to shut properly for some years, the shopkeeper reckoned people would guess the shop was open regardless of any sign. The few locals would know. It was almost the only 'mixed goods' shop for the next fifty miles. The settlement still had a garage and a butcher shop, left over from a gold rush mania long time gone.

The interior of the shop had a couple of tables and matching chairs, all from the same vintage with splayed legs. The tables had an aluminium strip screwed all-round the sides and over the edge of the Laminex which had bubbled up here and there. The shop's counter was levered towards the customer and made of a glass display cabinet which had a crack at the front, where at some earlier times efforts had been made with tape to try and prevent it from falling either out towards the floor or inwards towards the listless display of custard tarts, dry-looking Lamingtons, and some lonely mince pies. The tape was still holding on even if somewhat yellowed and curled. Against the back wall was another glass case with a bowl of floating beetroot slices and a plate holding sliced onions, while next were another couple of plates holding some limp artichokes with a hard boiled mess of what looked like chopped up eggs which had been sprinkled with Keens yellow curry powder. The Keens curry powder tin was still standing next to the plate, leaving open the optimistic possibility for future use. The ceiling was of pressed metal, bravely keeping some semblance to a floral pattern somewhat obscured by the numerous coats of paint applied through the decades. It was now painted a light hospital green and decorated with the hangings of three brown fly strip spirals that had lost its fatal attraction to anything in flight some years back. The whirring of a ceiling fan above the custard tarts glass case might have finally been installed to at least show the flies they were not all that welcome anymore. Besides, the health inspector had become somewhat grumpy and insisted the fan be installed, as well as a written direction to clear out the dead flies from the glass display cases.

The man put down his swag and back-pack outside, told the dog 'stay', which he instantly obeyed, squatting next to the swag. The dog was thirsty as well as hungry. After entering through the fly screen door, the solitary walker surveyed the interior and took in the sparsely filled shop. He knew that he could rely on a hamburger and cup of tea. The rancid smell of 50/50 hamburger mince and 100% lard had permeated floor, ceiling, furniture, not even giving the hard Laminex a chance in repelling it. The day had been hot. The walker's back-pack contained a small hoard of books as well as clothing. Dried fruit, including apricots and sliced apple, some nuts with a couple of bottles of water, completed the solitary walker's total inventory. The heat had weighed him down more than usual. He needed sustenance as well as to replenish water for himself and his dog. A woman appeared. She was dishevelled, hugely breasted and all crumpled. The TV blaring out with canned laughter from somewhere at the back indicated the possibility she might have been horizontally positioned when he entered the shop. He asked for a hamburger, a pot of tea and some water.

His daily walk in search of new and unread books had taken him longer than usual, and even though he passed several small settlements, none had books. His roving eyes had spotted shelving with frayed looking books just behind the tables facing the right hand wall away from the counter. His spirit lifted even before the hamburger arrived, which the shop-owner plonked on the fiery

Laminex table in the well-practiced and desultory manner of the country shop. She came in again and served a pot with cracked spout filled with hot water and a separate dusty tea bag and sugar and milk. She also, without wasting a single word, walked through the fly screen door with a dish of water for the dog outside. The Bluey dog was still camped next to his master's swag. His grateful slurping was heard inside with his dog-tag tinkling against the metal dish.

The man's thirst quenched by tea, the intrepid walker started on his well-layered hamburger, bits of beetroot trying to escape, slipping and sliding towards the edge which the solitary book searcher prevented them from falling by rotating the bread bun while expertly eating the protruding slices of guilty vegetables, including the brown rings of fried onions. The wandering book searcher had in the meantime surveyed the rag-tag of books on the shelving. He cast his eyes over the titles, holding his head askew this way and that, trying to read as much as was still visible on the torn covers. He munched approvingly on his rotating burger, now almost eaten to its core. His usual modus operandi was to exchange his quarry inside the back-pack for any unread ones. He mainly succeeded, especially if he traded two books for one. Depending on his limited finance he would just sometimes buy a book, a reckless splurge of the moment which so far he had never regretted. His need for books was till now still unrequited, dating back to childhood, deprived of letters and words printed on pages by an uncaring culture, and not made better by a bookless neighbourhood. He would never fill the void, but made up the deficit as good and as diligently as he was able. He was lucky to have been taught reading in the first place. He knew that if he was to catch up with books and the reading of them he could never waste time working for a living and money. He wanted to understand more of the world that he lived in. Time was of the essence, and because of that he could not afford wasting time in working for anything, let alone just money whose value could never be read.

His reading skill had been installed when very young in a faraway country of which he still had only vague memories. He remembered fondly that a distant uncle, rumoured to have emerged from a Tsarist Russian background and nobility, had taught him to play the mouth organ. He now had a small 'Hohner' organ with a button on the side for half-notes. His early childhood training had stood him in good stead despite the deprivations later when circumstance had transferred him to the relentless hot and dusty world he now resided in. When he arrived at a place that, through no intent of him, featured a market, he would put down his belongings, tell Bluey to 'sit', and start to play his mouth organ. He would only play long enough for people to provide him with enough coins for some future food and a frayed but unread book. He knew that by following a certain repertoire the coins would be dropped in his hat, especially during his playing of the very popular, 'When The Saints Come Marching In'. The combination of the music with Bluey's mournful looking eyes, cast upwards towards the audience; few would walk past without chucking a couple of pennies.

When the hamburger had finally been eaten and the last of the tea been squeezed and scored from the tea bag, our searcher stood up and paid for the food, including a couple of Spam-ham cans, making sure the cans still had the keys attached. He already knew that there was yet an unread book on the shelves that he badly wanted. He took a book from his backpack. It was a well-thumbed, 'The Brothers Karamazov'. He asked the large breasted shop-owner if he could swap this for the maroon coloured hard cover book on the top shelf. He also offered to top his offer up with a tuppence coin. She agreed, and offered him the use of the outhouse for a shower; 'That's if you want to shower, she asked. He, for a split second, thought there was something in the furtive way she looked sideways as she made the offer, away from his open gaze.

She knew the rule for wanderers with swags and cattle dogs. Itinerants, ring- barkers, fencers and shearers, they were the ones that she still managed to eke a living from. Some she befriended and even loved for a night or so, snatched away from the uncompromising hard fist of an otherwise solitary life, a life not unlike those that she sold her wares to. She hardly remembered her husband who had vanished without a grunt of a good-bye years ago. A hopeless drunk of piss-pot, he was. That's the most she recalled. Her solemn but generous giving of relief to the itinerant wanderers and flotsam of those on endless dirt roads cut both ways, and she preferred that to her previous marital mishap. Besides, it gave her business a chance to limp on.

After the swap to the maroon coloured book, 'Riders of the Chariot', he took up her offer of the shower at the back, but first went to the butchers for some bones for Bluey. This time it was a dishevelled male that served him. He was dressed in shorts and grimy singlet. 'Just some bones and lamb chops,' he asked. There were no books or shelving. Carcasses were dangling from hooks at the back wall and a compressor was busily trying to keep the room cool. The book searcher asked where the nearest town was; 'Somewhere with a market,' he said. 'Oodnadatta, fifty miles from here,' the butcher answered. 'Take plenty of water, but you might take a ride on the cattle train,' he advised. 'I have some water and food from the shop up the road,' the book searcher said. 'Taking a shower first?' the butcher asked, smiling back, with just a hint of something more, but left untold.

He got back, gave the bones to Bluey, who had patiently waited, confident his boss would not forget. Our wanderer, now satisfied with yet another book but still unwashed, went to the back of the shop for his shower. He undressed, and started to soap himself when the large breasted shop owner got through the door, offering him a towel as well as herself. She was naked but held her hands modestly before her large pendulous breasts. 'I'll soap your back,' she said. She pushed him against the wall. There was limited space, and the softness of her generous body pressed against his lean hardness was as good as any hot afternoon would ever get fifty miles from Oodnadatta, for him as well as her.

Afterwards, with the sun at four in the afternoon, our happy book searcher bade his goodbye and wandered to just outside the settlement. He spotted a large and lonely ghost gum. He spread his swag and told the dog, 'Sit'. He took out his Patrick White's, "Rider of the Chariot," and started his first page of his unread book.

"Who was that woman?" asked Mrs. Colquhoun, a rich lady who had come recently to live at Sarsaparilla. "Ah," Mrs. Sugden said, and laughed, "That was Miss Hare."

"She appears an unusual sort of person," Mrs. Colquhoun ventured to hope.

The Restless Book Searcher had found his book, yet again.

www.ingramcontent.com/pod-product-compliance
Lightning Source LLC
LaVergne TN
LVHW011218080426
835509LV00005B/201